CONTENTS

Published by ONDORISHA PUBLISHERS,LTD.
4 Tsukiji-machi,Shinjuku-ku,Tokyo,162-8708 Japan

First printing:April 2003
2nd printing:Sept.,2004

ISBN 4-88996-097-X   Printed in Japan

Distributors:
UNITED STATES:Kodansha America,Inc.through Oxford University Press,198 Madison Avenue,New York,NY 10016.
CANADA:Fitzhenry & Whiteside Ltd.,195 Allstate Parkway,Markham,Ontario L3R 4T8.
UNITED KINGDOM and EUROPE:Premier Book Marketing Ltd.,Clarendon House,52 Cornmarket Street,Oxford OX1 3HJ,England.
AUSTRALIA and NEW ZEALAND:Bookwise International, 54 Crittenden Road,Findon, South Australia 5023, Australia.
ASIA and JAPAN:Japan Publications Trading Co.,Ltd., 1-2-1 Sarugaku-cho,Chiyoda-ku, Tokyo,101-0064 Japan.

Rings

1

For your first project,why not make a ring? All you need are beads and fishing line.
The rings shown above combine faceted glass beads and pearl beads.
Instructions:#1→p.48

Rings...Neck.........Ensembles...Earrings...Straps...

2

To emphasize the design of these two rings with their voluminous tops, we have adopted a monochromatic color scheme. The ring at left is round, and the one at right is oval.

Instructions:#2→p.49 #3→p.50

3

Rings

4

Rings...Necklaces...Bracelets...Ensembles...Earrings...Straps...

We have chosen a simple design for this ring so that the focus is on the different types and colors of beads used. The rings on the opposite page are very easy to make. You simply form intersections between pearl beads and seed beads at regular intervals.

Instructions:#4,#5→p.51 #6→p.52

5

6

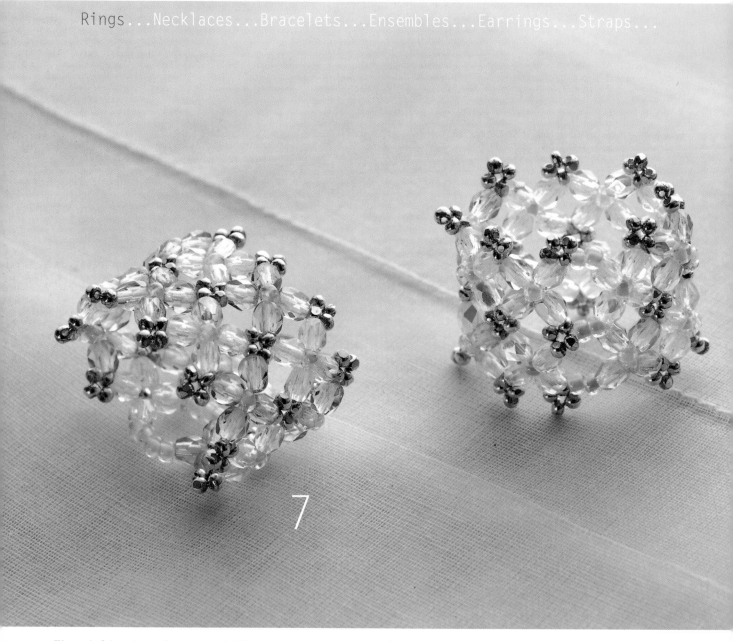

7

The delicate rings on this page are woven with oval faceted glass beads. We designed a matching pendant for the ring on the next page.
Instructions:#7→p.52 #8→p.80 #9→p.53

8

Rings

8

9

9

Rings

10

12

11

13

This ring features faceted glass beads woven into a sphere. It catches light from all directions each time you move your hand. The matching necklaces are based on the ring design, but are hemispheres rather than spheres.

Instructions:#10,#11→p.54 #12,#13→p.55

Necklaces

14

Tiny seed beads form the graceful curves of this elegant necklace.

Instructions:#14→p.56

Necklaces

15

16

17

14

Rings...Necklaces...Bracelets...Ensembles...Earrings...Straps...

These four necklaces are made with disc beads. The beads in two of them are connected with jump rings. The other two, one long and one short, have beads hanging from a chain, like fringe. The longer necklace is wound twice around the neck; it could also be worn as a belt.

Instructions:#15,#16→p.57 #17,#18→p.58

18

Rings...Necklaces...Bracelets...Ensembles...Earrings...Straps...

For the necklaces shown on this page, we used transparent beads, adding
colored faceted-glass bead accents.

Instructions:#19,#20→p.59

19

20

NeckIaces

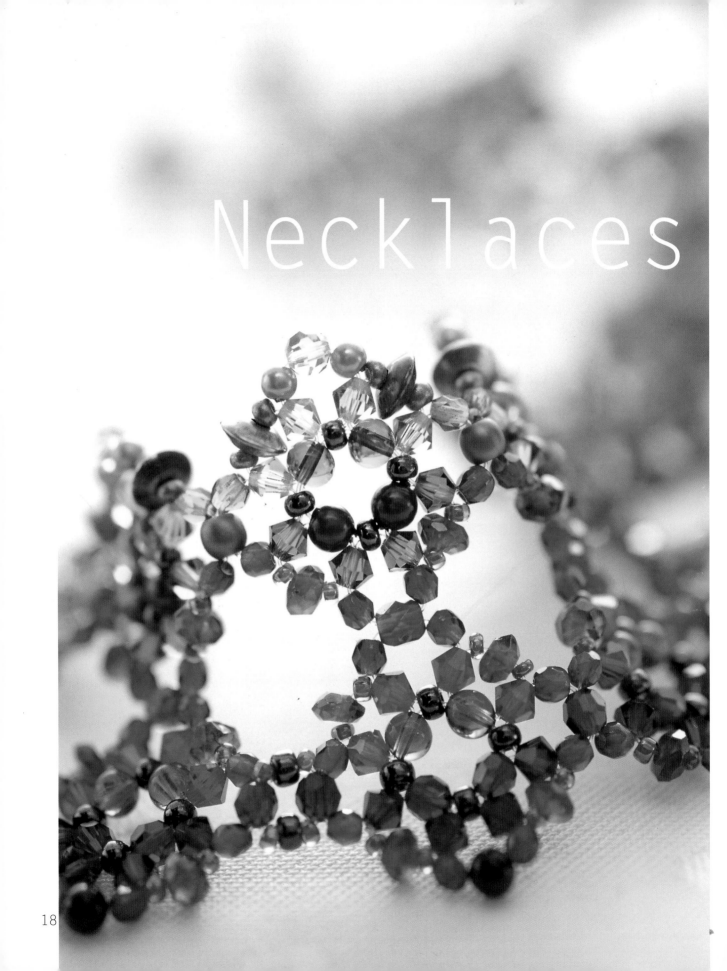

Necklaces

22

21

To make these two pieces, we combined several types of beads to form diamond shapes, which we then joined together. The necklace is curved to fit the contour of the throat. The clasps, which are also made from beads, add a wonderful finishing touch.

Instructions:#21→p.60 #22→p.61

23

25

24

26

We chose subdued colors for the necklaces and earrings pictured on these pages. To make #26, we strung beads on a wire choker. The necklace shown on the opposite page features rose beads.

Instructions:#23→p.80 #24,#25→p.62 #26,#27→p.63 #28,#29→p.64

Rings...Necklaces...Bracelets...Ensembles...Earrings...Straps...

Necklaces

28

27

29

21

Bracelets

30

This bracelet features candy-colored faceted glass beads woven in random order, and a bead clasp.

Instructions:#30→p.66

Rings...Necklaces...Bracelets...Ensembles...Earrings...Straps...

Wine-colored seed beads form a sophisticated backdrop for the bright-colored beads in this bracelet and matching earrings.

Instructions:#31→p.65 #32→p.66

31

32

Bracelets

Bracelets

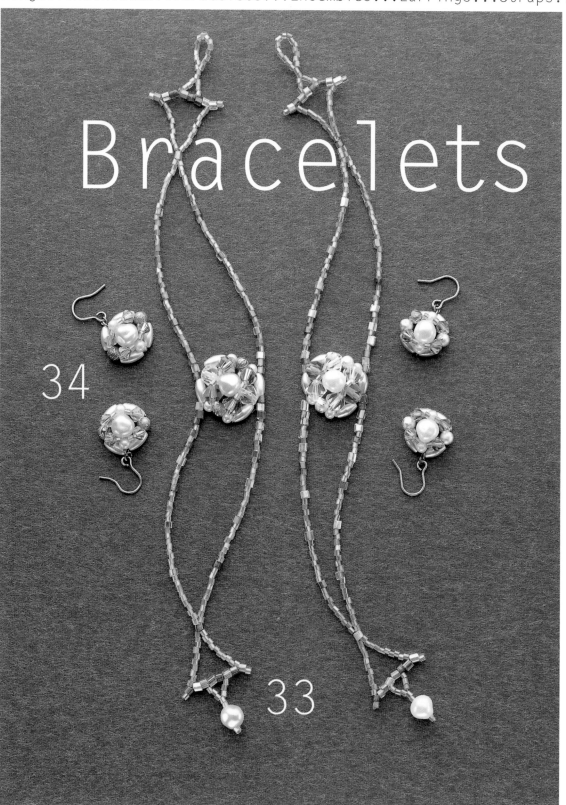

34

33

Large pearl beads are the centerpieces of these simple bracelets, which combine crystal, metal and smaller pearl beads. If you don't have pierced ears, just attach earring backs instead of ear wires.

Instructions:#33,#34→p.68

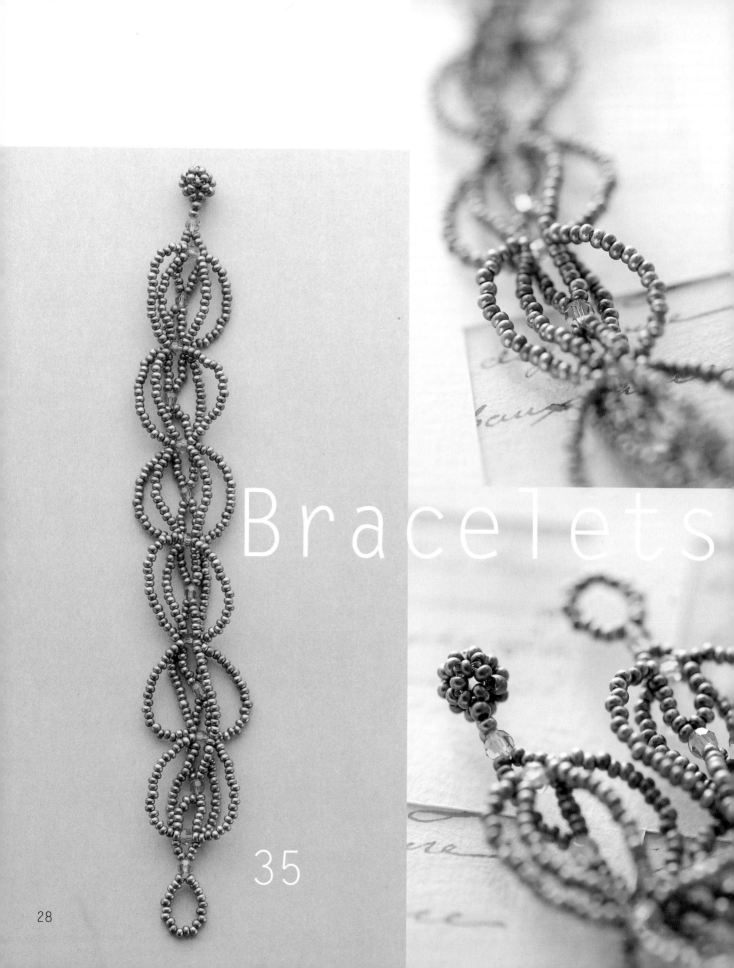

Bracelets

35

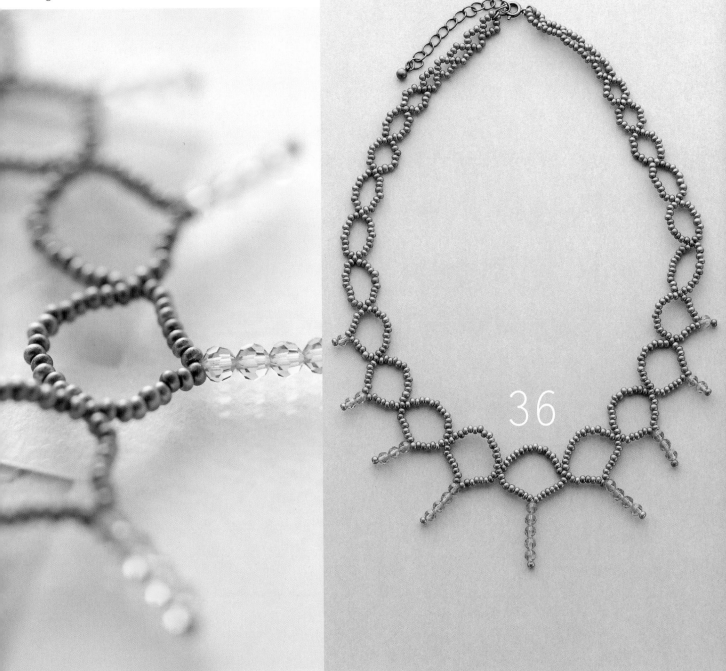

36

This bracelet and matching necklace are made from caramel-colored beads, but the overall effect is one of smoky gold.

Instructions:#35,#36→p.69

This bracelet and the matching fringed earrings are made with metallic and crystal beads
in soft,feminine colors.
Instructions:#37,#38→p.70

Bracelets

31

39

32

Flower motifs are the unifying features of this beautiful three-piece set
(necklace, bracelet and earrings).
Instructions:#39,#40→p.71 #41→p.72

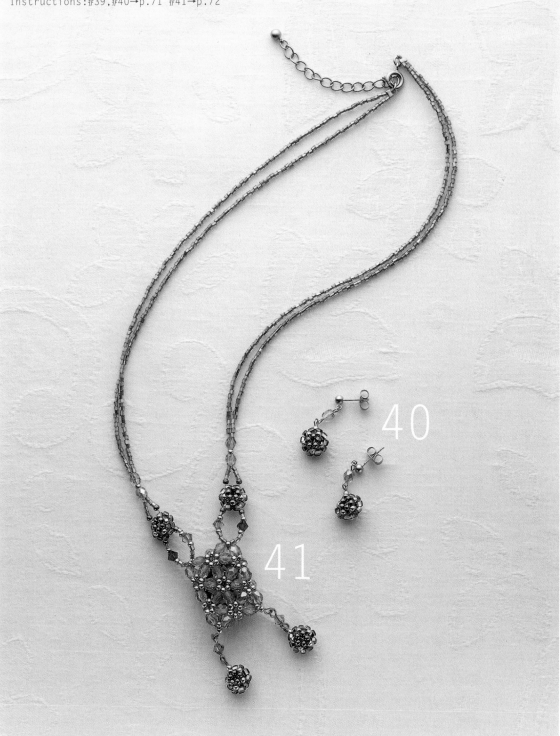

40

41

Ensembles

42

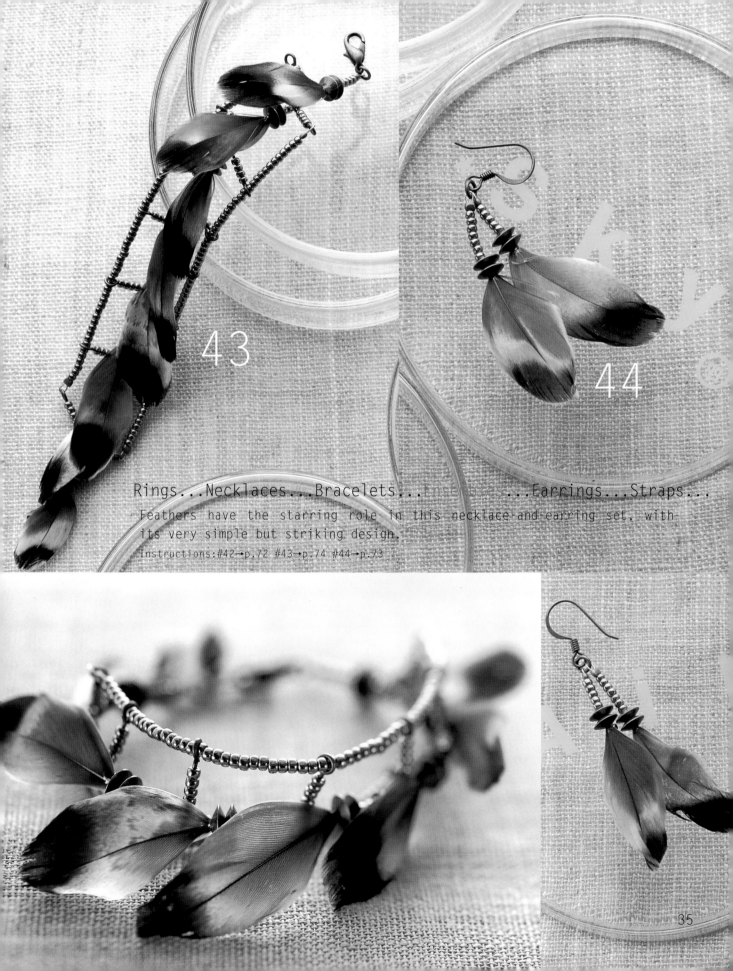

43

44

Rings...Necklaces...Bracelets...Insemble...Earrings...Straps...

Feathers have the starring role in this necklace-and-earring set, with its very simple but striking design.

Instructions:#42→p.72 #43→p.74 #44→p.73

To make this delicate necklace, feather-shaped motifs are attached to a row of strung beads, which is attached to another row of beads separated by beaded ribs. The bracelet is worked in a ladder pattern. The feather motifs in the necklace are repeated in the earrings.

Instructions:#45→p.74 #46→p.76 #47→p.77

47

46

45

nsembles

48

Earrings

The earrings on this page are made with headpins adorned with clusters of beads. The necklaces in the ensemble on the next page are worked in gradations of a main color. The earrings match the pendants on the necklaces.

Instructions:#48,#49→p.76 #50→p.77

49

Rings...Necklaces...Bracelets...Ensembles...Earrings...Straps...

50

51

Rings...Necklaces...Bracelets...Ensembles...Earrings...Straps...

These eyeglass chains are made mainly with seed beads, to which we added a few
faceted glass beads as accents. The cell-phone straps on the opposite page are
very easy to make for you just string the beads on fishing line.

Instructions:#51,#52→p.78 #53,#54→p.79

52

53

Straps

54

Instructions

Read the next five pages before you begin a project.

ABOUT BEADS

[Selecting beads]

Thanks to the recent revival of interest in beadcraft, beads are now available in a huge variety of styles and colors. They are also affordable, even though some of them could easily be mistaken for precious stones. In our instructions we supply bead sizes, but please feel free to use your favorite styles and colors to make an original piece of jewelry or accessory. For inspiration, visit your local bead or craft store.

[Purchasing beads]

In our instructions, we specify the exact number of beads needed to make each project. We do recommend, though, that you purchase a few extra beads, in case some get lost while you are working.

[Beginning a project]

Have small, flat containers, such as saucers, on hand to hold your beads. Place a solid-color piece of fabric (felt is ideal) on top of your work surface. Place the containers on top of the fabric, and empty the beads into them. You should be able to pick up the beads easily.

[While you work]

We have given you the finished measurements for each project, but you may need to make adjustments to allow for individual variations in neck and wrist length, or ring size. While you're working, try the piece on from time to time. If necessary, add or subtract beads.

[Caring for your beadwork]

Perspiration, dust and dirt will inevitably come in contact with anything you wear next to your skin. To prevent discoloration or deterioration of the beads, wipe the piece gently with a soft cloth every time you remove it from your body.

BASIC TOOLS

Shown on this page are the basic tools you will need to make the projects in this book.

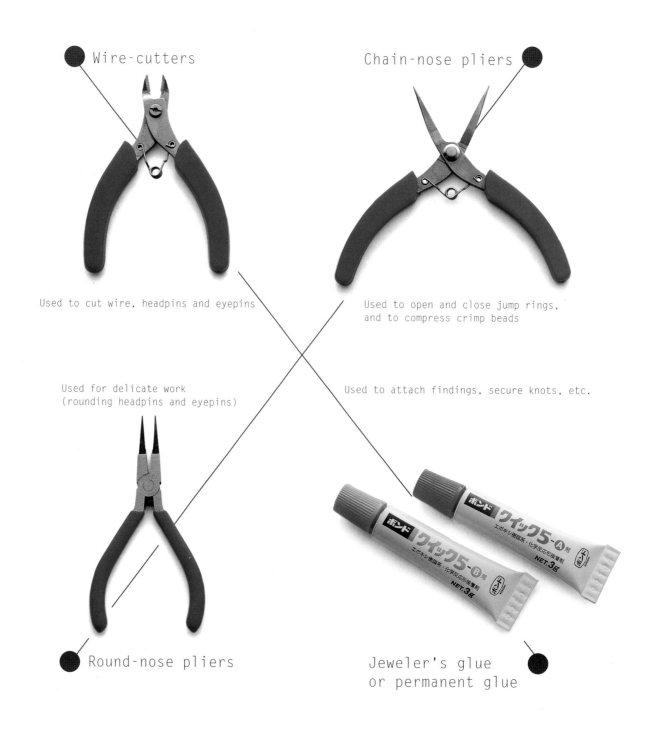

Wire-cutters

Chain-nose pliers

Used to cut wire, headpins and eyepins

Used to open and close jump rings,
and to compress crimp beads

Used for delicate work
(rounding headpins and eyepins)

Used to attach findings, secure knots, etc.

Round-nose pliers

Jeweler's glue
or permanent glue

SUPPLIES

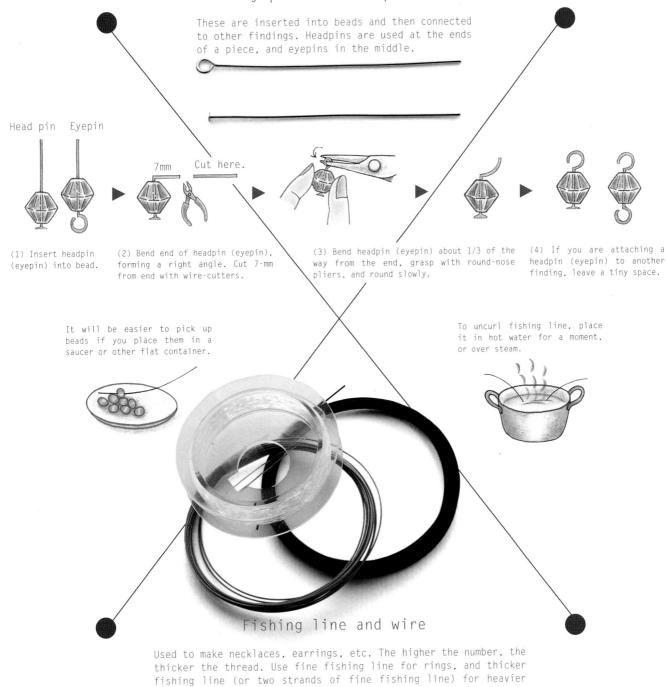

Eyepins and headpins

These are inserted into beads and then connected to other findings. Headpins are used at the ends of a piece, and eyepins in the middle.

Head pin   Eyepin

7mm   Cut here.

(1) Insert headpin (eyepin) into bead.

(2) Bend end of headpin (eyepin), forming a right angle. Cut 7-mm from end with wire-cutters.

(3) Bend headpin (eyepin) about 1/3 of the way from the end, grasp with round-nose pliers, and round slowly.

(4) If you are attaching a headpin (eyepin) to another finding, leave a tiny space.

It will be easier to pick up beads if you place them in a saucer or other flat container.

To uncurl fishing line, place it in hot water for a moment, or over steam.

Fishing line and wire

Used to make necklaces, earrings, etc. The higher the number, the thicker the thread. Use fine fishing line for rings, and thicker fishing line (or two strands of fine fishing line) for heavier pieces, such necklaces.

All wire used to make the accessories in this book is nylon wire.

 FINDINGS

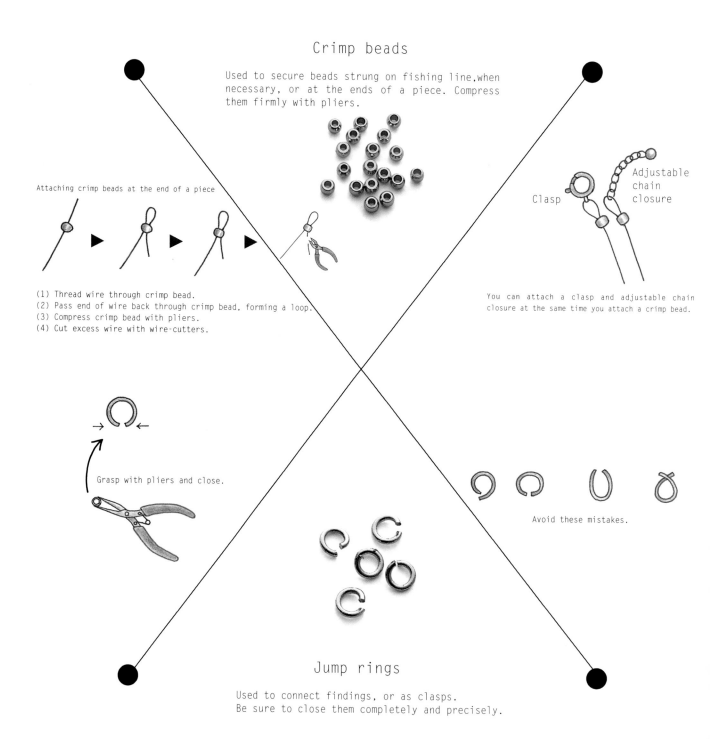

Crimp beads

Used to secure beads strung on fishing line,when necessary, or at the ends of a piece. Compress them firmly with pliers.

Attaching crimp beads at the end of a piece

(1) Thread wire through crimp bead.
(2) Pass end of wire back through crimp bead, forming a loop.
(3) Compress crimp bead with pliers.
(4) Cut excess wire with wire-cutters.

Clasp

Adjustable chain closure

You can attach a clasp and adjustable chain closure at the same time you attach a crimp bead.

Grasp with pliers and close.

Avoid these mistakes.

Jump rings

Used to connect findings, or as clasps.
Be sure to close them completely and precisely.

CLASPS

Clasps are attached to the ends
of bracelets and necklaces.

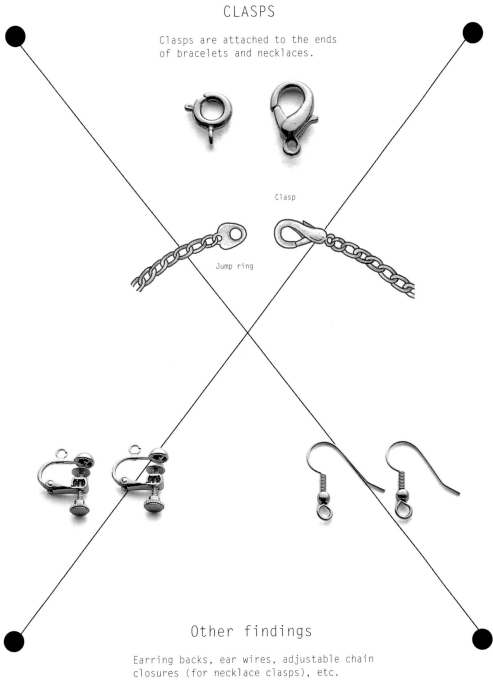

Clasp

Jump ring

Other findings

Earring backs, ear wires, adjustable chain
closures (for necklace clasps), etc.

#1
Ring
pp.2-3

Supplies: 8 3-mm faceted glass beads, 4-mm bicone beads (6 each beige and pink), 38 3-mm pearl beads, 52 1.4-mm seed beads, 24 1.9-mm seed beads, 150cm #3 fishing line

Instructions: 1. Make top of ring: String beads on center of fishing line, forming an intersection. Follow directions in drawings, ending with a row of seed beads. **2.** Make band, referring to drawings. Pass fishing line through a faceted glass bead on top of ring. Tie ends of fishing line together, hide in beads, and cut excess.

Dimensions: 5.5cm (inside diameter)

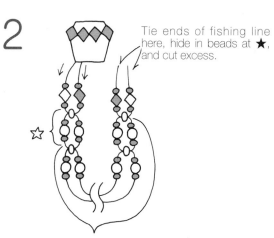

2

Tie ends of fishing line here, hide in beads at ★, and cut excess.

Repeat ☆ six times.

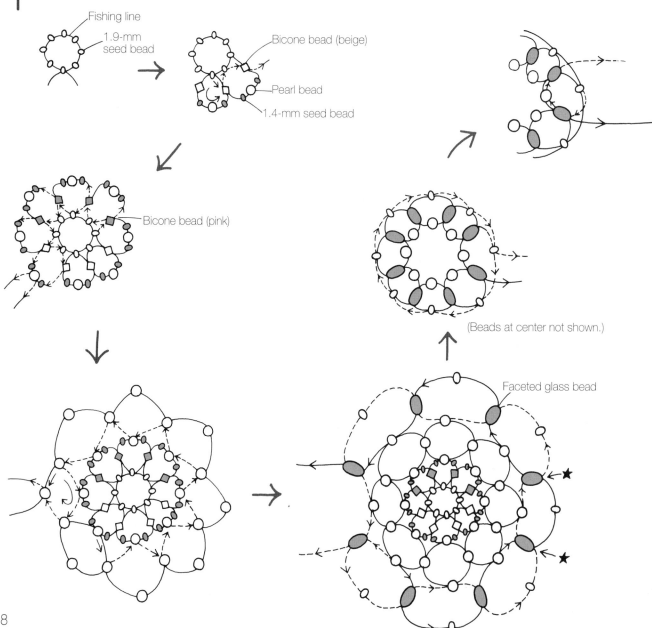

1

Fishing line

1.9-mm seed bead

Bicone bead (beige)

Pearl bead

1.4-mm seed bead

Bicone bead (pink)

(Beads at center not shown.)

Faceted glass bead

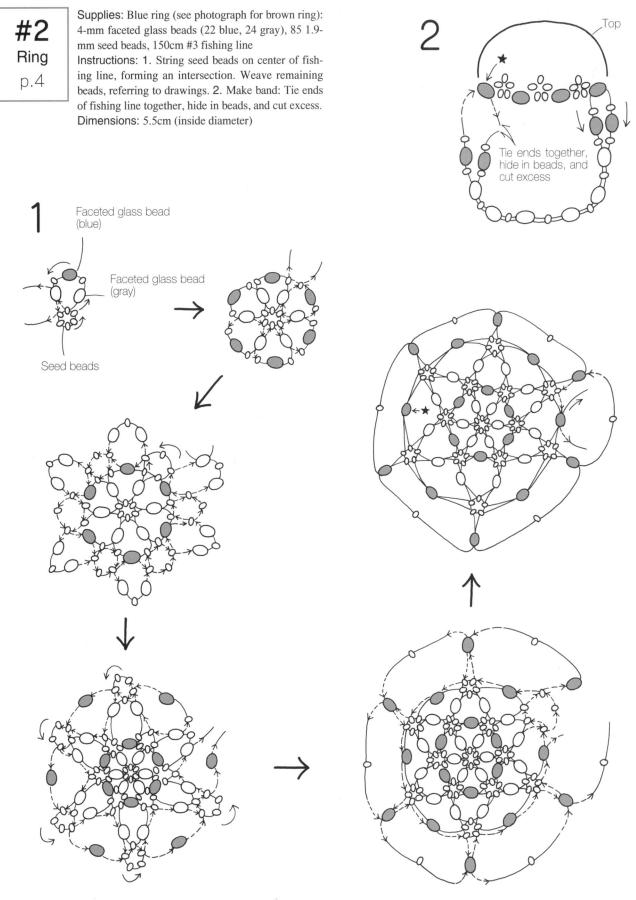

#2
Ring
p.4

Supplies: Blue ring (see photograph for brown ring): 4-mm faceted glass beads (22 blue, 24 gray), 85 1.9-mm seed beads, 150cm #3 fishing line

Instructions: 1. String seed beads on center of fishing line, forming an intersection. Weave remaining beads, referring to drawings. **2.** Make band: Tie ends of fishing line together, hide in beads, and cut excess.

Dimensions: 5.5cm (inside diameter)

2

Top

Tie ends together, hide in beads, and cut excess

1

Faceted glass bead (blue)

Faceted glass bead (gray)

Seed beads

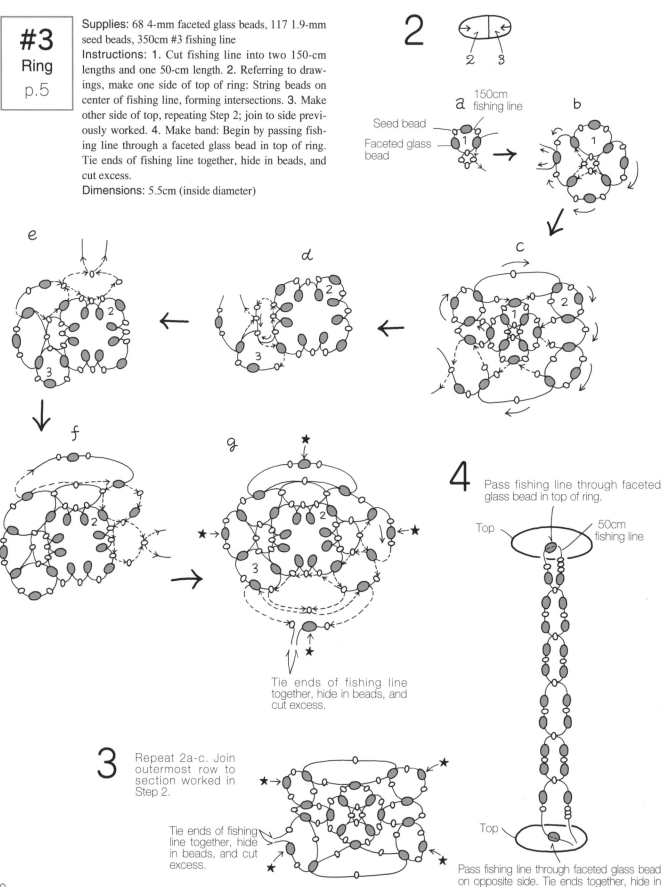

#3 Ring
p.5

Supplies: 68 4-mm faceted glass beads, 117 1.9-mm seed beads, 350cm #3 fishing line

Instructions: 1. Cut fishing line into two 150-cm lengths and one 50-cm length. **2.** Referring to drawings, make one side of top of ring: String beads on center of fishing line, forming intersections. **3.** Make other side of top, repeating Step 2; join to side previously worked. **4.** Make band: Begin by passing fishing line through a faceted glass bead in top of ring. Tie ends of fishing line together, hide in beads, and cut excess.

Dimensions: 5.5cm (inside diameter)

2

a 150cm fishing line

Seed bead

Faceted glass bead

b

c

d

e

f

g

Tie ends of fishing line together, hide in beads, and cut excess.

3 Repeat 2a-c. Join outermost row to section worked in Step 2.

Tie ends of fishing line together, hide in beads, and cut excess.

4 Pass fishing line through faceted glass bead in top of ring.

Top

50cm fishing line

Top

Pass fishing line through faceted glass bead on opposite side. Tie ends together, hide in beads, and cut excess.

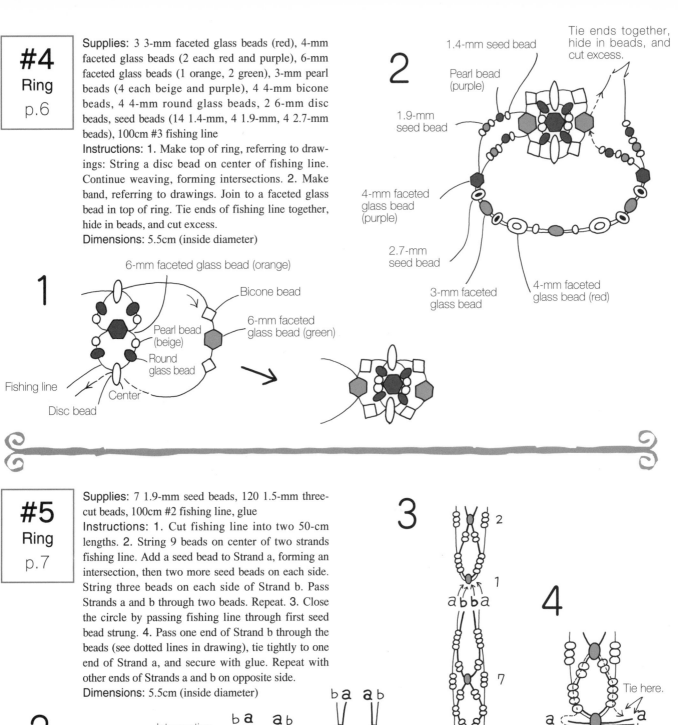

#4 Ring
p.6

Supplies: 3 3-mm faceted glass beads (red), 4-mm faceted glass beads (2 each red and purple), 6-mm faceted glass beads (1 orange, 2 green), 3-mm pearl beads (4 each beige and purple), 4 4-mm bicone beads, 4 4-mm round glass beads, 2 6-mm disc beads, seed beads (14 1.4-mm, 4 1.9-mm, 4 2.7-mm beads), 100cm #3 fishing line

Instructions: 1. Make top of ring, referring to drawings: String a disc bead on center of fishing line. Continue weaving, forming intersections. 2. Make band, referring to drawings. Join to a faceted glass bead in top of ring. Tie ends of fishing line together, hide in beads, and cut excess.

Dimensions: 5.5cm (inside diameter)

2

- 1.4-mm seed bead
- Pearl bead (purple)
- 1.9-mm seed bead
- 4-mm faceted glass bead (purple)
- 2.7-mm seed bead
- 3-mm faceted glass bead
- 4-mm faceted glass bead (red)

Tie ends together, hide in beads, and cut excess.

1

- 6-mm faceted glass bead (orange)
- Bicone bead
- Pearl bead (beige)
- 6-mm faceted glass bead (green)
- Round glass bead
- Fishing line
- Center
- Disc bead

#5 Ring
p.7

Supplies: 7 1.9-mm seed beads, 120 1.5-mm three-cut beads, 100cm #2 fishing line, glue

Instructions: 1. Cut fishing line into two 50-cm lengths. 2. String 9 beads on center of two strands fishing line. Add a seed bead to Strand a, forming an intersection, then two more seed beads on each side. String three beads on each side of Strand b. Pass Strands a and b through two beads. Repeat. 3. Close the circle by passing fishing line through first seed bead strung. 4. Pass one end of Strand b through the beads (see dotted lines in drawing), tie tightly to one end of Strand a, and secure with glue. Repeat with other ends of Strands a and b on opposite side.

Dimensions: 5.5cm (inside diameter)

3

a b b a   1
2
7
6

4

Tie here.
a b   a
b

※ If you have trouble passing the fishing line through a bead, enlarge the hole with a needle.

2

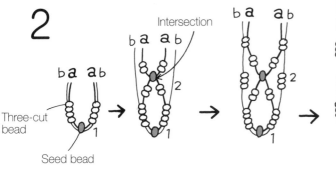

- Three-cut bead
- Seed bead
- Intersection

b a a b   1
b a a b   2   1
b a a b   3   2   1
b a a b   2   1

Repeat.

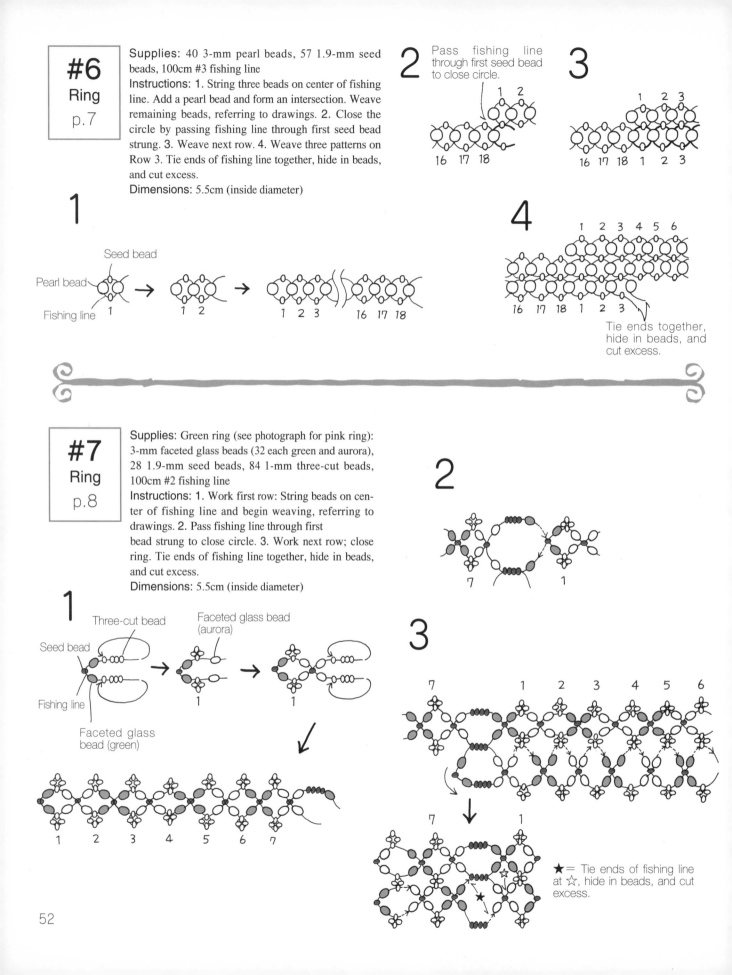

#6 Ring p.7

Supplies: 40 3-mm pearl beads, 57 1.9-mm seed beads, 100cm #3 fishing line

Instructions: 1. String three beads on center of fishing line. Add a pearl bead and form an intersection. Weave remaining beads, referring to drawings. 2. Close the circle by passing fishing line through first seed bead strung. 3. Weave next row. 4. Weave three patterns on Row 3. Tie ends of fishing line together, hide in beads, and cut excess.

Dimensions: 5.5cm (inside diameter)

2 Pass fishing line through first seed bead to close circle.

1 2

16 17 18

3

1 2 3

16 17 18 1 2 3

1

Seed bead

Pearl bead

Fishing line

1 → 1 2 → 1 2 3 16 17 18

4

1 2 3 4 5 6

16 17 18 1 2 3

Tie ends together, hide in beads, and cut excess.

#7 Ring p.8

Supplies: Green ring (see photograph for pink ring): 3-mm faceted glass beads (32 each green and aurora), 28 1.9-mm seed beads, 84 1-mm three-cut beads, 100cm #2 fishing line

Instructions: 1. Work first row: String beads on center of fishing line and begin weaving, referring to drawings. 2. Pass fishing line through first bead strung to close circle. 3. Work next row; close ring. Tie ends of fishing line together, hide in beads, and cut excess.

Dimensions: 5.5cm (inside diameter)

2

7 1

1

Three-cut bead

Faceted glass bead (aurora)

Seed bead

Fishing line

Faceted glass bead (green)

1   1

1 2 3 4 5 6 7

3

7 1 2 3 4 5 6

7 1

★ = Tie ends of fishing line at ☆, hide in beads, and cut excess.

52

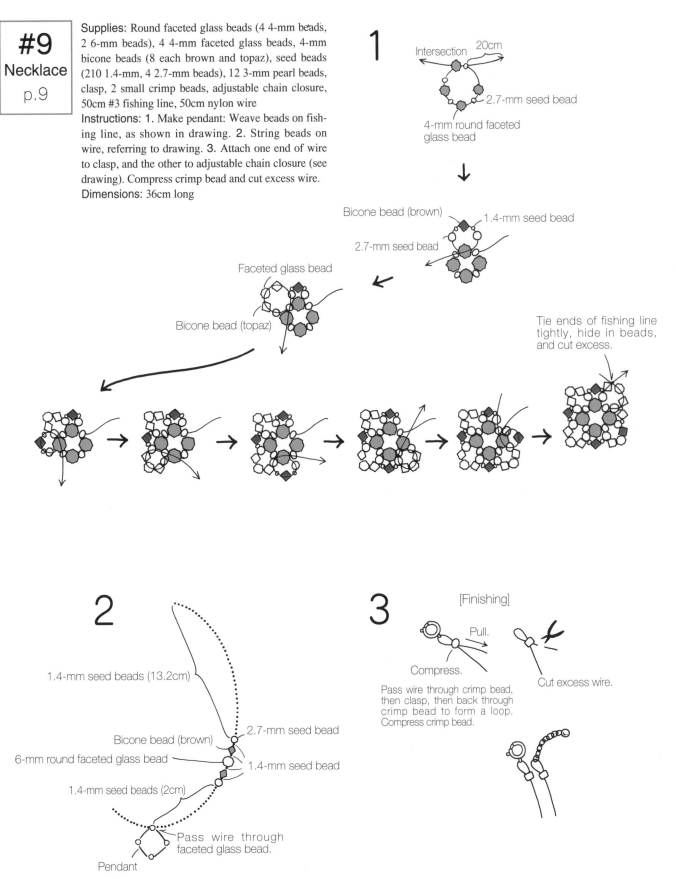

#9
Necklace
p.9

Supplies: Round faceted glass beads (4 4-mm beads, 2 6-mm beads), 4 4-mm faceted glass beads, 4-mm bicone beads (8 each brown and topaz), seed beads (210 1.4-mm, 4 2.7-mm beads), 12 3-mm pearl beads, clasp, 2 small crimp beads, adjustable chain closure, 50cm #3 fishing line, 50cm nylon wire

Instructions: 1. Make pendant: Weave beads on fishing line, as shown in drawing. 2. String beads on wire, referring to drawing. 3. Attach one end of wire to clasp, and the other to adjustable chain closure (see drawing). Compress crimp bead and cut excess wire.

Dimensions: 36cm long

1

Intersection 20cm

2.7-mm seed bead

4-mm round faceted glass bead

Bicone bead (brown) 1.4-mm seed bead
2.7-mm seed bead

Faceted glass bead

Bicone bead (topaz)

Tie ends of fishing line tightly, hide in beads, and cut excess.

2

1.4-mm seed beads (13.2cm)

Bicone bead (brown) 2.7-mm seed bead

6-mm round faceted glass bead 1.4-mm seed bead

1.4-mm seed beads (2cm)

Pass wire through faceted glass bead.

Pendant

3 [Finishing]

Pull.

Compress.

Cut excess wire.

Pass wire through crimp bead, then clasp, then back through crimp bead to form a loop. Compress crimp bead.

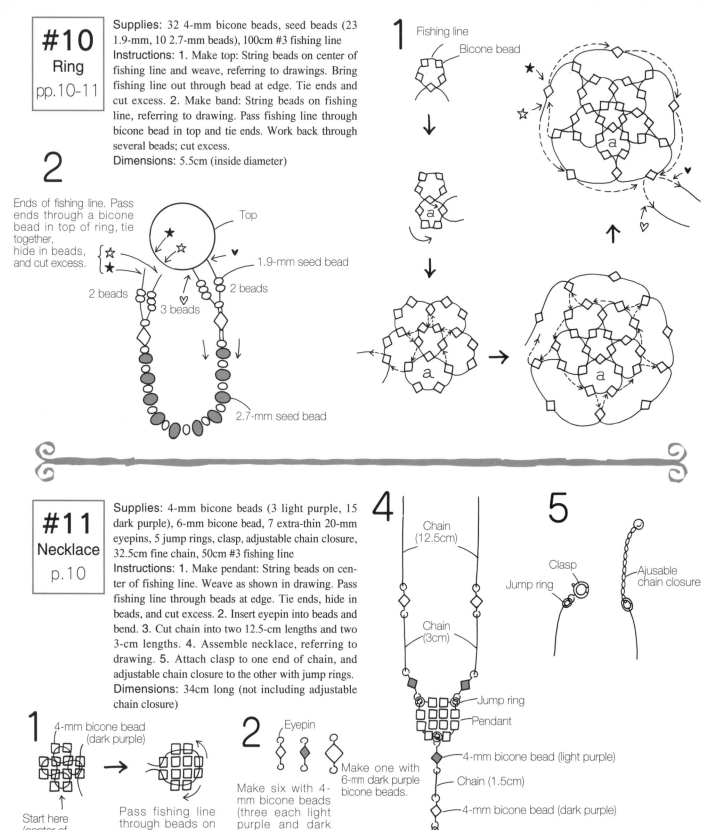

#10 Ring
pp.10-11

Supplies: 32 4-mm bicone beads, seed beads (23 1.9-mm, 10 2.7-mm beads), 100cm #3 fishing line

Instructions: 1. Make top: String beads on center of fishing line and weave, referring to drawings. Bring fishing line out through bead at edge. Tie ends and cut excess. **2. Make band:** String beads on fishing line, referring to drawing. Pass fishing line through bicone bead in top and tie ends. Work back through several beads; cut excess.

Dimensions: 5.5cm (inside diameter)

1

Fishing line
Bicone bead

2

Ends of fishing line. Pass ends through a bicone bead in top of ring, tie together, hide in beads, and cut excess.

Top
1.9-mm seed bead
2 beads
2 beads
3 beads
2.7-mm seed bead

#11 Necklace
p.10

Supplies: 4-mm bicone beads (3 light purple, 15 dark purple), 6-mm bicone bead, 7 extra-thin 20-mm eyepins, 5 jump rings, clasp, adjustable chain closure, 32.5cm fine chain, 50cm #3 fishing line

Instructions: 1. Make pendant: String beads on center of fishing line. Weave as shown in drawing. Pass fishing line through beads at edge. Tie ends, hide in beads, and cut excess. **2.** Insert eyepin into beads and bend. **3.** Cut chain into two 12.5-cm lengths and two 3-cm lengths. **4.** Assemble necklace, referring to drawing. **5.** Attach clasp to one end of chain, and adjustable chain closure to the other with jump rings.

Dimensions: 34cm long (not including adjustable chain closure)

1

4-mm bicone bead (dark purple)

Start here (center of fishing line).

Pass fishing line through beads on perimeter of pendant. Pull tight, tie ends, hide in beads, and cut excess.

2

Eyepin

Make six with 4-mm bicone beads (three each light purple and dark purple).

Make one with 6-mm dark purple bicone beads.

4

Chain (12.5cm)
Chain (3cm)
Jump ring
Pendant
4-mm bicone bead (light purple)
Chain (1.5cm)
4-mm bicone bead (dark purple)
6-mm bicone bead

5

Clasp
Jump ring
Ajusable chain closure

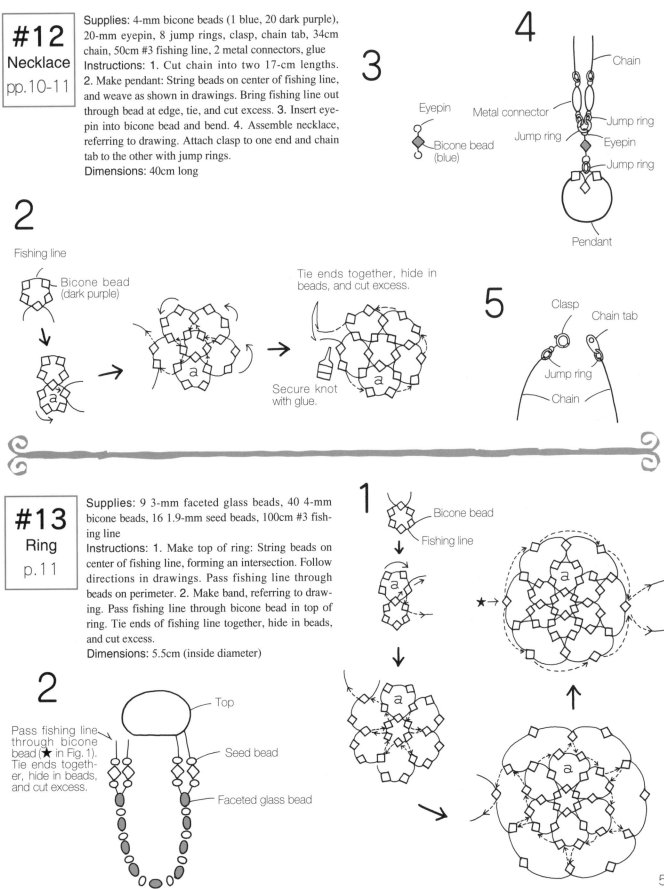

#12
Necklace
pp.10-11

Supplies: 4-mm bicone beads (1 blue, 20 dark purple), 20-mm eyepin, 8 jump rings, clasp, chain tab, 34cm chain, 50cm #3 fishing line, 2 metal connectors, glue
Instructions: 1. Cut chain into two 17-cm lengths. 2. Make pendant: String beads on center of fishing line, and weave as shown in drawings. Bring fishing line out through bead at edge, tie, and cut excess. 3. Insert eyepin into bicone bead and bend. 4. Assemble necklace, referring to drawing. Attach clasp to one end and chain tab to the other with jump rings.
Dimensions: 40cm long

3

Eyepin

Bicone bead
(blue)

4

Chain

Metal connector

Jump ring

Jump ring

Eyepin

Jump ring

Pendant

2

Fishing line

Bicone bead
(dark purple)

a

a

Tie ends together, hide in beads, and cut excess.

Secure knot with glue.

a

5

Clasp

Chain tab

Jump ring

Chain

#13
Ring
p.11

Supplies: 9 3-mm faceted glass beads, 40 4-mm bicone beads, 16 1.9-mm seed beads, 100cm #3 fishing line
Instructions: 1. Make top of ring: String beads on center of fishing line, forming an intersection. Follow directions in drawings. Pass fishing line through beads on perimeter. 2. Make band, referring to drawing. Pass fishing line through bicone bead in top of ring. Tie ends of fishing line together, hide in beads, and cut excess.
Dimensions: 5.5cm (inside diameter)

1

Bicone bead

Fishing line

a

★→

a

a

a

2

Pass fishing line through bicone bead (★ in Fig. 1). Tie ends together, hide in beads, and cut excess.

Top

Seed bead

Faceted glass bead

55

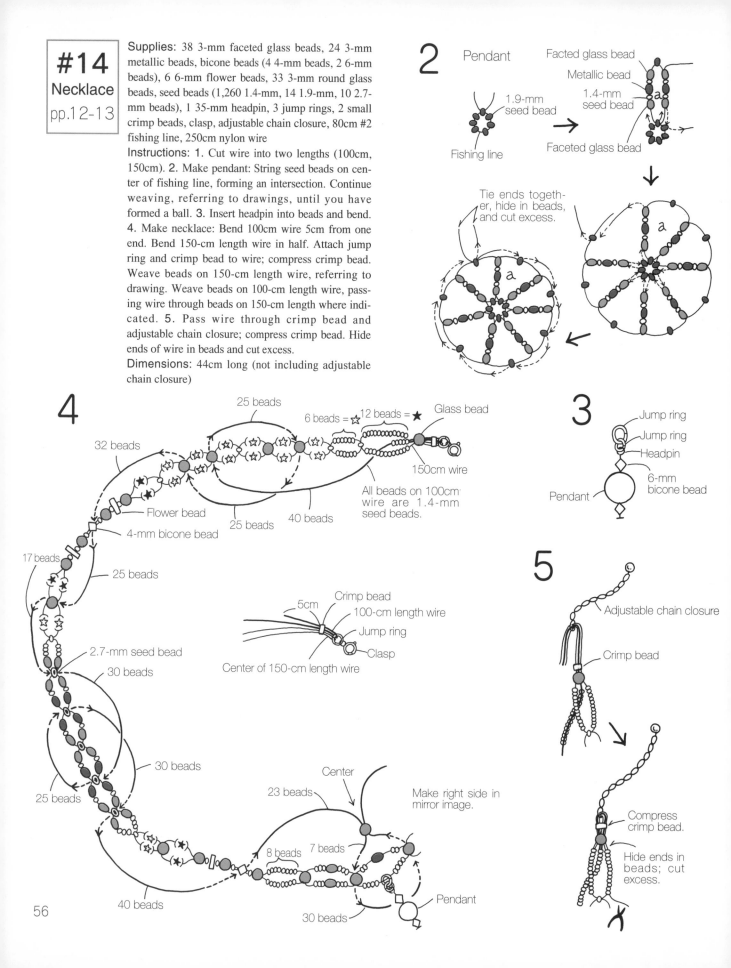

#14 Necklace
pp.12-13

Supplies: 38 3-mm faceted glass beads, 24 3-mm metallic beads, bicone beads (4 4-mm beads, 2 6-mm beads), 6 6-mm flower beads, 33 3-mm round glass beads, seed beads (1,260 1.4-mm, 14 1.9-mm, 10 2.7-mm beads), 1 35-mm headpin, 3 jump rings, 2 small crimp beads, clasp, adjustable chain closure, 80cm #2 fishing line, 250cm nylon wire

Instructions: 1. Cut wire into two lengths (100cm, 150cm). **2.** Make pendant: String seed beads on center of fishing line, forming an intersection. Continue weaving, referring to drawings, until you have formed a ball. **3.** Insert headpin into beads and bend. **4.** Make necklace: Bend 100cm wire 5cm from one end. Bend 150-cm length wire in half. Attach jump ring and crimp bead to wire; compress crimp bead. Weave beads on 150-cm length wire, referring to drawing. Weave beads on 100-cm length wire, passing wire through beads on 150-cm length where indicated. **5.** Pass wire through crimp bead and adjustable chain closure; compress crimp bead. Hide ends of wire in beads and cut excess.

Dimensions: 44cm long (not including adjustable chain closure)

2 Pendant

1.9-mm seed bead

Fishing line

Facted glass bead
Metallic bead
1.4-mm seed bead
a
Faceted glass bead

Tie ends together, hide in beads, and cut excess.

a

3
Jump ring
Jump ring
Headpin
6-mm bicone bead
Pendant

4
25 beads
6 beads = ☆   12 beads = ★
Glass bead
32 beads
All beads on 100cm wire are 1.4-mm seed beads.
150cm wire
Flower bead
4-mm bicone bead
25 beads
40 beads
17 beads
25 beads
2.7-mm seed bead
30 beads
30 beads
25 beads
40 beads

Center
23 beads
Make right side in mirror image.
8 beads
7 beads
Pendant
30 beads

5cm
Crimp bead
100-cm length wire
Jump ring
Clasp
Center of 150-cm length wire

5
Adjustable chain closure
Crimp bead

Compress crimp bead.
Hide ends in beads; cut excess.

#15 Necklace p.14

Supplies: Beige necklace (see photograph for blue necklace): 1.3-cm shell disc beads (13 green, 25 gold, 26 black beads with two holes; 1 gold bead with one hole), 71 jump rings, clasp
Instructions: Connect beads and clasp with jump rings, referring to drawing.
Dimensions: 77-84cm long

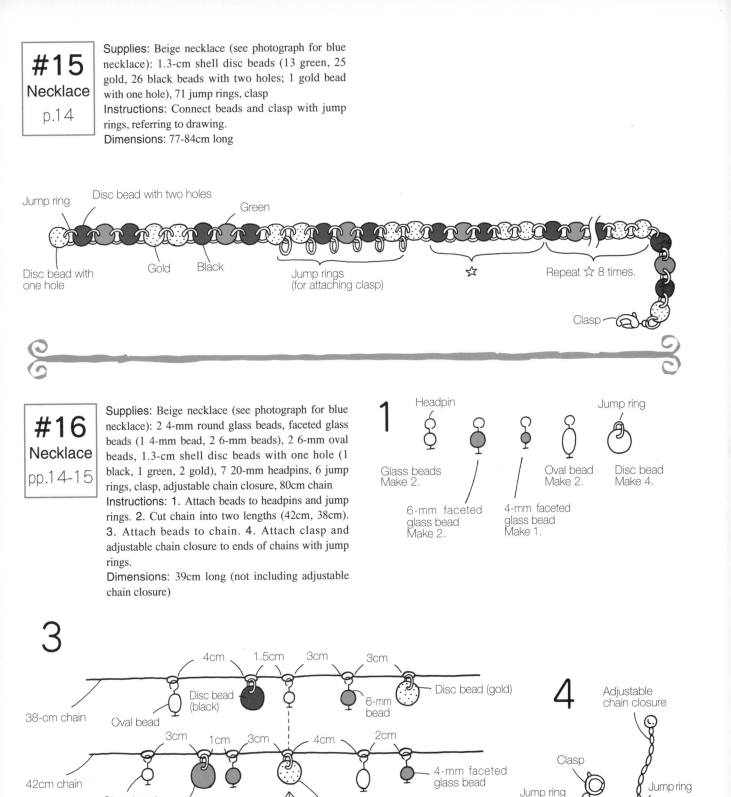

Jump ring

Disc bead with two holes

Green

Disc bead with one hole

Gold   Black

Jump rings (for attaching clasp)

☆   Repeat ☆ 8 times.

Clasp

#16 Necklace pp.14-15

Supplies: Beige necklace (see photograph for blue necklace): 2 4-mm round glass beads, faceted glass beads (1 4-mm bead, 2 6-mm beads), 2 6-mm oval beads, 1.3-cm shell disc beads with one hole (1 black, 1 green, 2 gold), 7 20-mm headpins, 6 jump rings, clasp, adjustable chain closure, 80cm chain
Instructions: 1. Attach beads to headpins and jump rings. 2. Cut chain into two lengths (42cm, 38cm). 3. Attach beads to chain. 4. Attach clasp and adjustable chain closure to ends of chains with jump rings.
Dimensions: 39cm long (not including adjustable chain closure)

1

Headpin

Jump ring

Glass beads
Make 2.

6-mm faceted glass bead Make 2.

4-mm faceted glass bead Make 1.

Oval bead Make 2.

Disc bead Make 4.

3

4cm   1.5cm   3cm   3cm

Disc bead (black)

6-mm bead

Disc bead (gold)

38-cm chain   Oval bead

3cm   1cm   3cm   4cm   2cm

42cm chain

Glass bead

Disc bead (green)

Center

Disc bead (gold)

4-mm faceted glass bead

4

Adjustable chain closure

Clasp

Jump ring   Jump ring

#17
Necklace
p.14

Supplies: 3 4-mm round glass beads, 2 6-mm faceted glass beads, 2 6-mm oval beads, 1.3-cm shell disc beads with one hole (3 green, 4 each dark blue and white), 7 20-mm headpins, 15 jump rings, clasp, 120cm chain

Instructions: 1. Attach beads to headpins and jump rings. 2. Cut chain into two lengths (86cm, 34cm). 3. Attach beads to 86-cm chain, referring to drawing. 4. Join ends of 86-cm chain with jump ring. Attach clasp to one end of 34-cm chain with jump ring. Attach jump ring to other end, and join to jump ring on 86-cm chain.

Dimensions: 78cm long

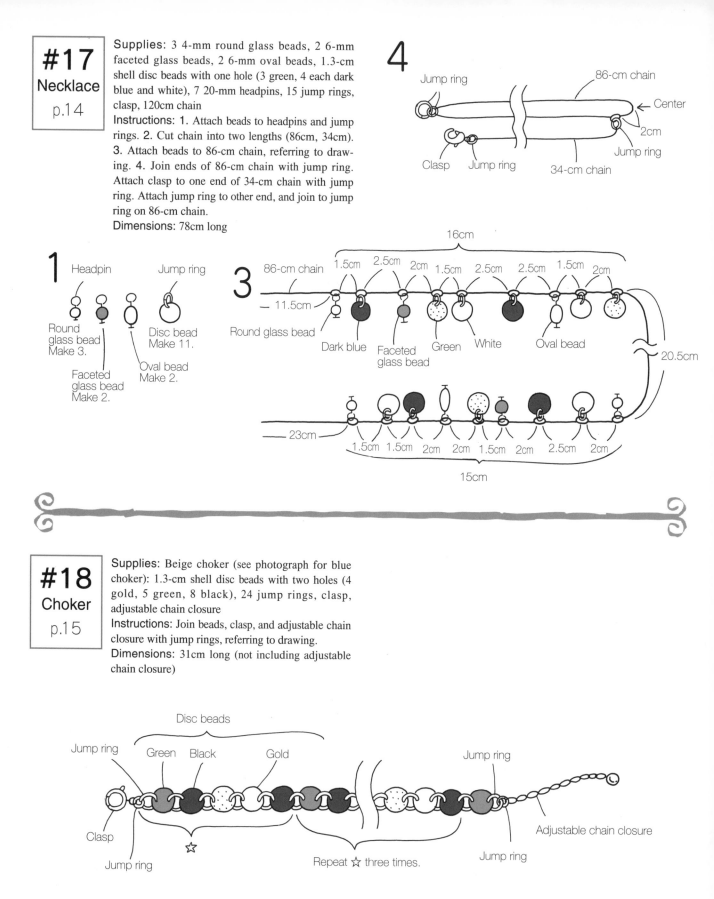

4
Jump ring
86-cm chain
← Center
2cm
Jump ring
Clasp   Jump ring
34-cm chain

1
Headpin
Jump ring
Round glass bead Make 3.
Faceted glass bead Make 2.
Oval bead Make 2.
Disc bead Make 11.

3
86-cm chain
11.5cm
Round glass bead
16cm
1.5cm 2.5cm 2cm 1.5cm 2.5cm 2.5cm 1.5cm 2cm
Dark blue Faceted glass bead Green White Oval bead
20.5cm
23cm
1.5cm 1.5cm 2cm 2cm 1.5cm 2cm 2.5cm 2cm
15cm

#18
Choker
p.15

Supplies: Beige choker (see photograph for blue choker): 1.3-cm shell disc beads with two holes (4 gold, 5 green, 8 black), 24 jump rings, clasp, adjustable chain closure

Instructions: Join beads, clasp, and adjustable chain closure with jump rings, referring to drawing.

Dimensions: 31cm long (not including adjustable chain closure)

Disc beads
Jump ring
Green Black Gold
Jump ring
Clasp
Jump ring
☆
Repeat ☆ three times.
Jump ring
Adjustable chain closure

58

#19 Necklace pp.16-17

Supplies: 3 6-mm round faceted glass beads, 4 4-mm faceted glass beads, 4 6-mm beads faceted glass beads, 180 2-mm square beads, 2.7-mm round seed bead, 9 3-mm pearl beads, 20-mm headpin, jump ring, clasp, chain tab, 2 small crimp beads, 50cm nylon wire

Instructions: 1. Insert headpin into beads. Bend and attach to jump ring, as shown in drawing. 2. String beads on wire. 3. Attach a crimp bead to each end of the wire. Hide ends of wire in beads, and cut excess.

Dimensions: 37cm long

3 [Finishing]

Compress crimp bead.

Pass wire through crimp bead, then clasp, then back through crimp bead, forming a loop. Compress crimp bead with pliers.

Cut excess wire.

1

Head pin — Jump ring
Pearl bead
Round faceted glass bead

[How to bend headpins and eyepins]

Headpin   Eyepin

① Insert headpin (eyepin) into hole in bead.

② 7mm Cut here. Bend headpin (eyepin) at a right angle; cut 7mm from end.

③ Grasp headpin (eyepin) with pliers about 1/3 of the way between bead and end; round slowly.

④ If joining headpin (eyepin) to other components, leave a small space.

2

Square beads (12-14cm)

Pearl bead
Round faceted glass bead
4-mm faceted glass bead
Square beads (1)
Square beads (10)
6-mm faceted glass bead

Form intersection at round seed bead.

When you form intersections, pull wire tightly to attain desired shape.

Square beads (2)
Start here.
Drop (see Fig.1)

#20 Necklace pp.16-17

Supplies: 5 4-mm round beads, 4-mm round faceted glass beads (5 each garnet and blue), 180 2.7-mm seed beads, 2 jump rings, 14 crimp beads, clasp, bead tip, 180cm #4 fishing line

Instructions: 1. Cut fishing line. 2. String beads on three strands fishing line, referring to drawing. 3. Gather ends of fishing line and attach bead tip. Piece should measure 20cm from center to bead tip. 4. Attach clasp to hook in bead tip with jump ring.

Dimensions: 39cm long

[How to use bead tips]

① Pass three strands fishing line through bead tip. Tie a knot at base of bead tip with the aid of a needle or other pointed object..

② Cut here. Tie tightly, two or three times, to secure. Apply glue to knot.

③ Close bead tip and cut excess fishing line.

2~4

Pass all three strands fishing line through this bead.
Jump ring
Clasp
Bead tip
Seed beads
5 beads on each strand
Pass all three strands through these beads.
Crimp bead (compress with pliers)
Round faceted glass bead (garnet)
Round bead
Round faceted glass bead (blue)

String beads in mirror image, starting at center.

Center

59

Supplies: 4-mm round faceted glass beads (13 beige, 52 red), 13 4-mm oval faceted glass beads, 3-mm faceted glass beads (26 orange, 156 red), 78 4-mm disc-shaped faceted glass beads, 4-mm bicone beads (52 each brown, beige, red, dark red), 4-mm pearl beads (13 black, 26 purple), 26 3-mm pearl beads, 4-mm round glass beads (26 each brown and purple), 26 6-mm disc beads, 2 4-mm metallic beads, 1.4-mm seed beads (30 each orange and red), 1.9-mm seed beads (44 matte reddish-gold, 96 matte gold, 204 pink), 2.7-mm seed beads (52 gold, 76 purple), 14 4-mm round beads, 10m #3 fishing line

Instructions: 1. Make ball clasp: String seed beads on center of fishing line, forming an intersection. Continue weaving, referring to drawings. 2. Make Row 1 of choker: Beginning with matte gold clasp, string beads as shown in drawing, forming intersections. 3. Make Row 2 of choker: Beginning with reddish-gold clasp, repeat instructions for Row 1, joining 4-mm oval faceted glass beads to Row 1. 4. After you have woven 13 patterns, make loops at ends of Rows 1 and 2, referring to drawings. Tie two strands of fishing line together, hide in beads, and cut excess.

※Cut fishing line into 200-cm lengths; add a new length when you need it.

Dimensions: 34cm long

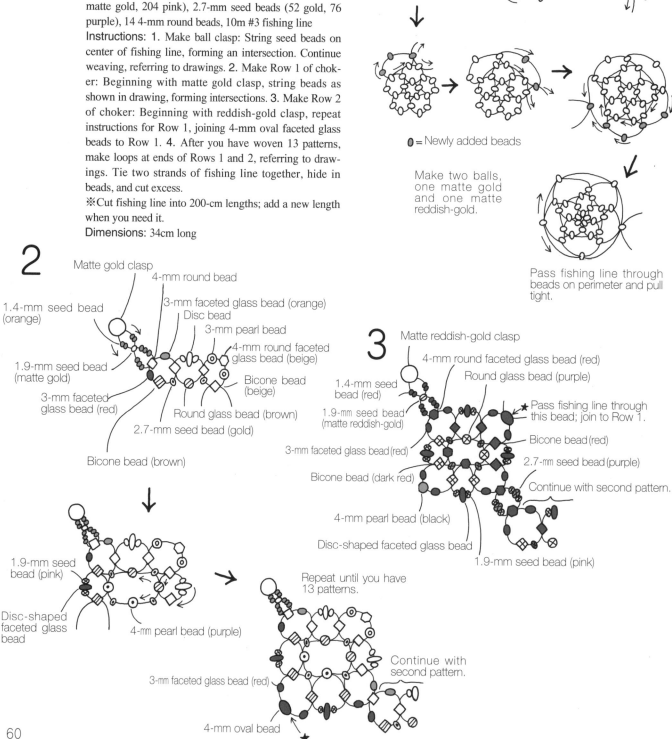

1

1.9-mm seed beads
Center of fishing line

𝟘 = Newly added beads

Make two balls, one matte gold and one matte reddish-gold.

Pass fishing line through beads on perimeter and pull tight.

2

Matte gold clasp
4-mm round bead
3-mm faceted glass bead (orange)
1.4-mm seed bead (orange)
Disc bead
3-mm pearl bead
4-mm round faceted glass bead (beige)
1.9-mm seed bead (matte gold)
Bicone bead (beige)
3-mm faceted glass bead (red)
Round glass bead (brown)
2.7-mm seed bead (gold)
Bicone bead (brown)

1.9-mm seed bead (pink)
Disc-shaped faceted glass bead
4-mm pearl bead (purple)
3-mm faceted glass bead (red)
4-mm oval bead

3

Matte reddish-gold clasp
4-mm round faceted glass bead (red)
Round glass bead (purple)
1.4-mm seed bead (red)
1.9-mm seed bead (matte reddish-gold)
★ Pass fishing line through this bead; join to Row 1.
3-mm faceted glass bead (red)
Bicone bead (red)
Bicone bead (dark red)
2.7-mm seed bead (purple)
Continue with second pattern.
4-mm pearl bead (black)
Disc-shaped faceted glass bead
1.9-mm seed bead (pink)

Repeat until you have 13 patterns.

Continue with second pattern.

#22 Bracelet
pp.18-19

Supplies: 4-mm round faceted glass beads (5 beige, 16 red), 5 4-mm oval faceted glass beads, 3-mm faceted glass beads (10 orange, 60 red), 30 4-mm disc-shaped faceted glass beads, 4-mm bicone beads (20 each brown, beige, red, dark red), 10 3-mm pearl beads, 4-mm pearl beads (5 black, 10 purple), 4-mm round glass beads (10 each brown and purple), 10 6-mm disc beads, 4 4-mm metallic beads, 1.4-mm seed beads (30 each orange and red), 1.9-mm seed beads (45 matte reddish-gold, 60 pink, 65 matte gold), 2.7-mm seed beads (20 each gold and purple), 6 4-mm round beads, 500cm #3 fishing line

Instructions: 1. Cut fishing line into two 250-cm lengths. Follow directions for choker on p. 60. (Make clasp, then work Rows 1 and 2.) 2. Weave beads, forming intersections, as shown in drawing. 3. Make loops, tie ends of fishing line, hide in beads, and cut excess.

Dimensions: 15.5cm long

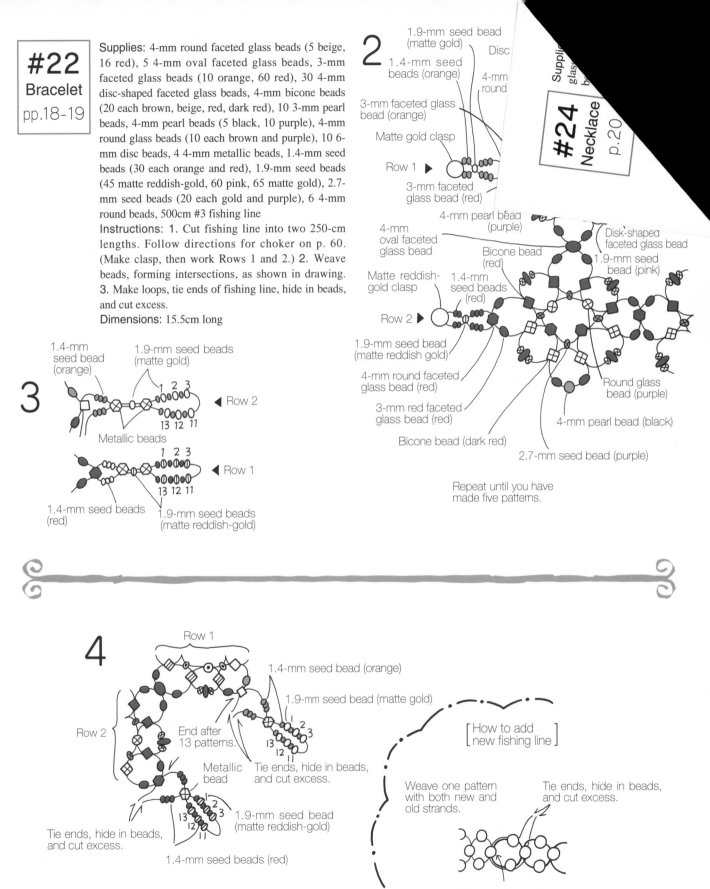

2

1.9-mm seed bead (matte gold)

Disc

1.4-mm seed beads (orange)

4-mm round

3-mm faceted glass bead (orange)

Matte gold clasp

Row 1 ▶

3-mm faceted glass bead (red)

4-mm pearl bead (purple)

Disk-shaped faceted glass bead

4-mm oval faceted glass bead

Bicone bead (red)

1.9-mm seed bead (pink)

Matte reddish-gold clasp

1.4-mm seed beads (red)

Row 2 ▶

1.9-mm seed bead (matte reddish gold)

4-mm round faceted glass bead (red)

3-mm red faceted glass bead (red)

Bicone bead (dark red)

Round glass bead (purple)

4-mm pearl bead (black)

2.7-mm seed bead (purple)

Repeat until you have made five patterns.

#24 Necklace p.20

3

1.4-mm seed bead (orange)

1.9-mm seed beads (matte gold)

1 2 3

◀ Row 2

13 12 11

Metallic beads

1 2 3

◀ Row 1

13 12 11

1.4-mm seed beads (red)

1.9-mm seed beads (matte reddish-gold)

4

Row 1

1.4-mm seed bead (orange)

1.9-mm seed bead (matte gold)

1 2 3

Row 2

13 12 11

End after 13 patterns.

Metallic bead

Tie ends, hide in beads, and cut excess.

1.9-mm seed bead (matte reddish-gold)

Tie ends, hide in beads, and cut excess.

1.4-mm seed beads (red)

1 2 3

13 12 11

[How to add new fishing line]

Weave one pattern with both new and old strands.

Tie ends, hide in beads, and cut excess.

Center of fishing line

...es: 6-mm faceted glass bead, 4-mm faceted ... beads (8 light gray, 14 gray), 4-mm bicone ...ead, 23 2.7-mm seed beads, 15-mm headpin, 5 20-mm eyepins, 12 jump rings, clasp, adjustable chain closure, 120cm #2 fishing line

Instructions: 1. Make pendant: String 6 seed beads on center of fishing line, forming an inter-section. Continue weaving, referring to drawings. Tie ends of fishing line, hide in beads, and cut excess. **2.** Insert headpin and eyepins into beads and bend. **3.** Cut chain into two 12.5-cm lengths and five 1.2-cm lengths. Assemble necklace, refer-ring to drawings. **4.** Attach clasp and adjustable chain closure to ends of chain with jump rings.

Dimensions: 33cm long (not including adjustable chain closure)

2 Headpin
Seed bead — Make 1.
6-mm faceted glass bead

3 12.5-cm chain
Light gray
Jump ring
Gray
4-mm faceted glass beads

4-mm faceted glass beads
Gray — Light gray
Eyepin
Jump ring
Bicone bead
Seed bead
Make 1. Make 2 of each.

4 Clasp — Adjustable chain closure
Jump ring
1.2-cm chain

Pendant
1.2-cm chain
Jump ring
Bicone bead
6-mm faceted glass bead

1 Fishing line
Seed bead
4-mm faceted glass beads
Gray — Light gray

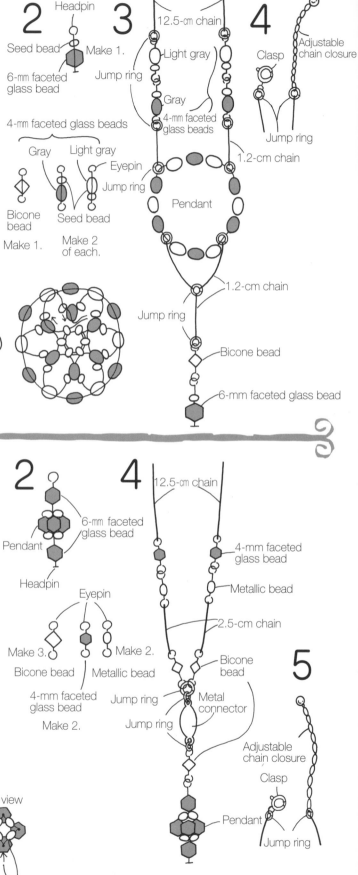

#25 Necklace p.20

Supplies: 6 6-mm faceted glass beads, 2 4-mm faceted glass beads, 3 4-mm bicone beads, 10 4-mm metallic beads, 1.2-cm flat decorative connector, 35-mm headpin, 7 15-mm eyepins, 5 jump rings, clasp, adjustable chain closure, 30cm chain, 50cm #2 fishing line

Instructions: 1. Make pendant: String three beads on center of fishing line, followed by a faceted glass bead, forming an intersection. Continue weaving, referring to drawings. Close circle by passing fishing line through first faceted glass bead. Pass one end of fishing line through faceted glass bead once more to meet other end. Tie ends, hide in beads, and cut excess. **2.** Insert headpin, eyepin, and two additional beads into pendant. Bend ends of pins. **3.** Cut chain into two 12.5-cm lengths and two 2.5-cm lengths. **4.** Assemble necklace, referring to drawings. **5.** Attach clasp and adjustable chain closure to ends of chain with jump rings.

Dimensions: 40cm long (not including adjustable chain closure)

2 6-mm faceted glass bead
Pendant
Headpin

Eyepin
Make 3. Make 2.
Bicone bead Metallic bead
4-mm faceted glass bead
Make 2.

4 12.5-cm chain
4-mm faceted glass bead
Metallic bead
2.5-cm chain
Bicone bead
Jump ring
Metal connector
Jump ring
Pendant

5 Adjustable chain closure
Clasp
Jump ring

1 Metallic bead — Top view
6-mm faceted glass bead

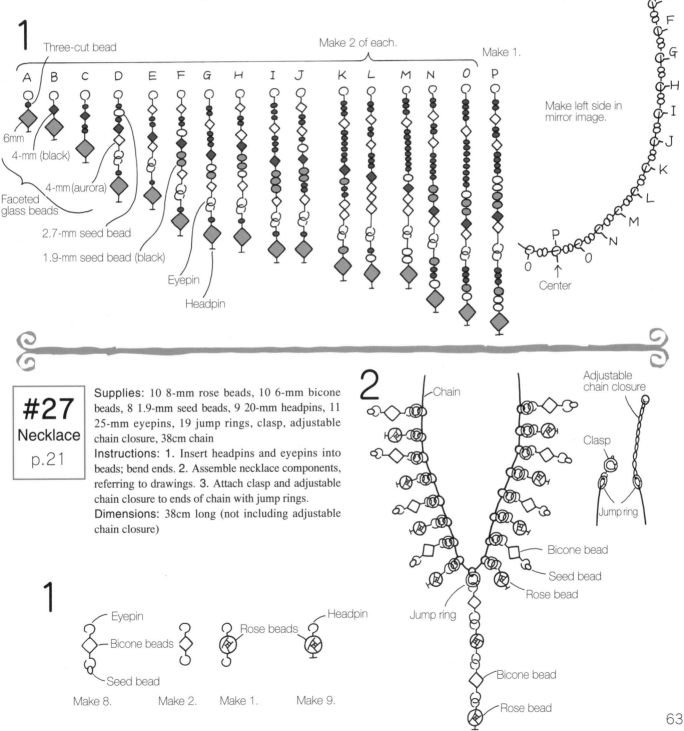

#26 Choker p.20

Supplies: 31 6-mm faceted glass beads, 4-mm faceted glass beads (29 black, 65 aurora), 1.9-mm seed beads (60 gray, 39 black), 28 2.7-mm seed beads, 193 1.5-mm three-cut beads, 31 25-mm headpins, 4 25-mm eyepins, 8 35-mm eyepins, 13 45-mm eyepins, wire choker

Instructions: 1. Insert eyepins and headpins into beads; bend ends. 2. String components on wire choker, alternating with two seed beads.

Dimensions: 33cm long

1

Three-cut bead

Make 2 of each.

Make 1.

A B C D E F G H I J K L M N O P

6mm

4-mm (black)

4-mm (aurora)

Faceted glass beads

2.7-mm seed bead

1.9-mm seed bead (black)

Eyepin

Headpin

2

Wire choker

1.9-mm seed beads (gray)

A B C D E F G H I J K L M N

Make left side in mirror image.

P

O O

Center

#27 Necklace p.21

Supplies: 10 8-mm rose beads, 10 6-mm bicone beads, 8 1.9-mm seed beads, 9 20-mm headpins, 11 25-mm eyepins, 19 jump rings, clasp, adjustable chain closure, 38cm chain

Instructions: 1. Insert headpins and eyepins into beads; bend ends. 2. Assemble necklace components, referring to drawings. 3. Attach clasp and adjustable chain closure to ends of chain with jump rings.

Dimensions: 38cm long (not including adjustable chain closure)

2

Chain

Adjustable chain closure

Clasp

Jump ring

Bicone bead

Seed bead

Rose bead

Jump ring

Bicone bead

Rose bead

1

Eyepin

Bicone beads

Seed bead

Make 8.

Make 2.

Rose beads

Make 1.

Headpin

Make 9.

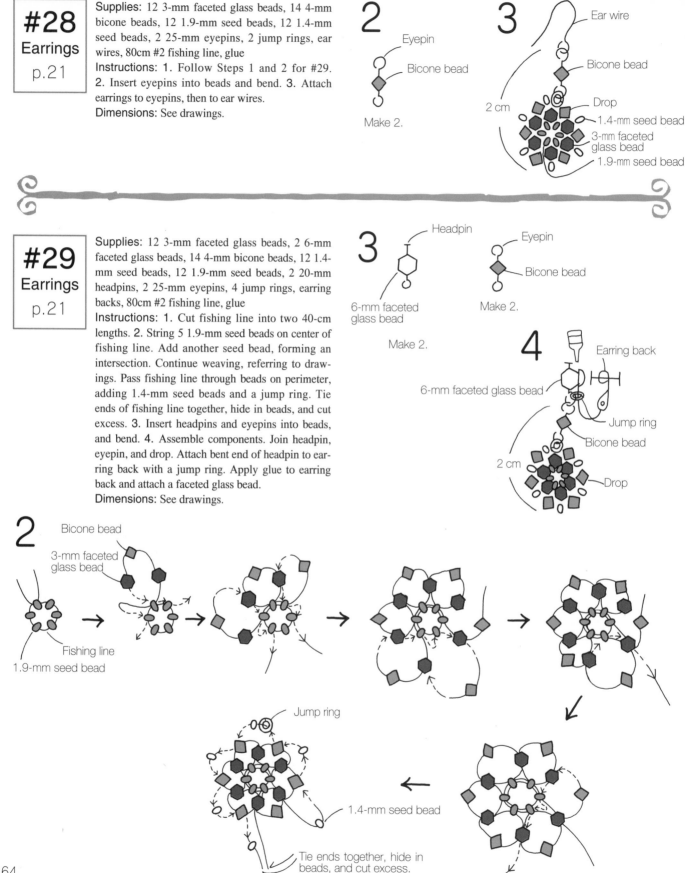

#28 Earrings p.21

Supplies: 12 3-mm faceted glass beads, 14 4-mm bicone beads, 12 1.9-mm seed beads, 12 1.4-mm seed beads, 2 25-mm eyepins, 2 jump rings, ear wires, 80cm #2 fishing line, glue
Instructions: 1. Follow Steps 1 and 2 for #29. 2. Insert eyepins into beads and bend. 3. Attach earrings to eyepins, then to ear wires.
Dimensions: See drawings.

2
Eyepin
Bicone bead
Make 2.

3
Ear wire
Bicone bead
2 cm
Drop
1.4-mm seed bead
3-mm faceted glass bead
1.9-mm seed bead

#29 Earrings p.21

Supplies: 12 3-mm faceted glass beads, 2 6-mm faceted glass beads, 14 4-mm bicone beads, 12 1.4-mm seed beads, 12 1.9-mm seed beads, 2 20-mm headpins, 2 25-mm eyepins, 4 jump rings, earring backs, 80cm #2 fishing line, glue
Instructions: 1. Cut fishing line into two 40-cm lengths. 2. String 5 1.9-mm seed beads on center of fishing line. Add another seed bead, forming an intersection. Continue weaving, referring to drawings. Pass fishing line through beads on perimeter, adding 1.4-mm seed beads and a jump ring. Tie ends of fishing line together, hide in beads, and cut excess. 3. Insert headpins and eyepins into beads, and bend. 4. Assemble components. Join headpin, eyepin, and drop. Attach bent end of headpin to earring back with a jump ring. Apply glue to earring back and attach a faceted glass bead.
Dimensions: See drawings.

3
Headpin
6-mm faceted glass bead
Make 2.

Eyepin
Bicone bead
Make 2.

4
Earring back
6-mm faceted glass bead
Jump ring
Bicone bead
2 cm
Drop

2
Bicone bead
3-mm faceted glass bead
Fishing line
1.9-mm seed bead

Jump ring
1.4-mm seed bead
Tie ends together, hide in beads, and cut excess.

64

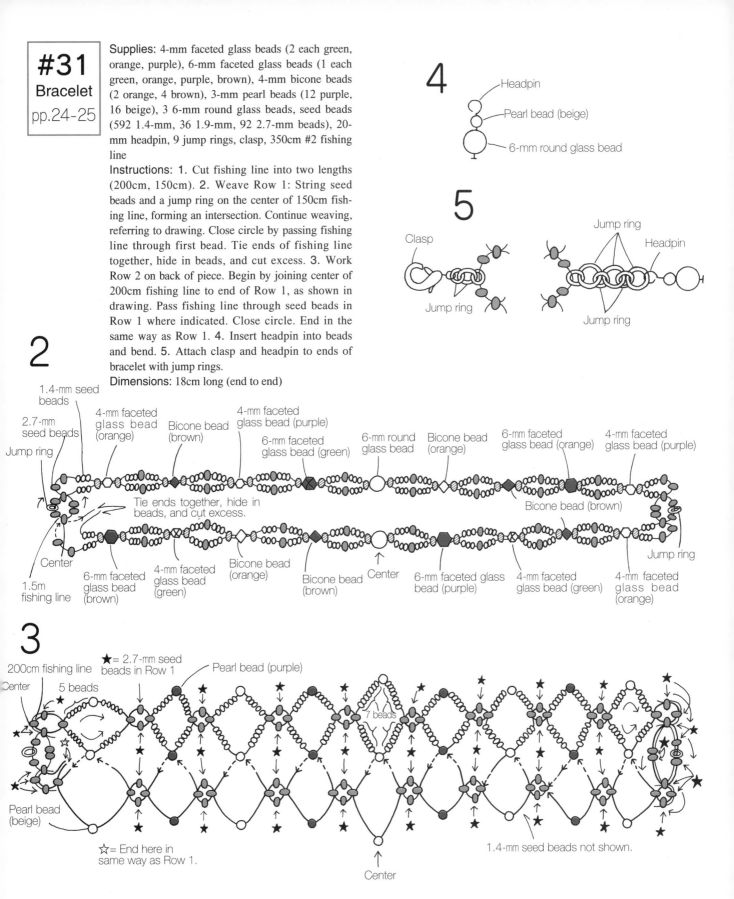

#31 Bracelet
pp.24-25

Supplies: 4-mm faceted glass beads (2 each green, orange, purple), 6-mm faceted glass beads (1 each green, orange, purple, brown), 4-mm bicone beads (2 orange, 4 brown), 3-mm pearl beads (12 purple, 16 beige), 3 6-mm round glass beads, seed beads (592 1.4-mm, 36 1.9-mm, 92 2.7-mm beads), 20-mm headpin, 9 jump rings, clasp, 350cm #2 fishing line

Instructions: 1. Cut fishing line into two lengths (200cm, 150cm). **2.** Weave Row 1: String seed beads and a jump ring on the center of 150cm fishing line, forming an intersection. Continue weaving, referring to drawing. Close circle by passing fishing line through first bead. Tie ends of fishing line together, hide in beads, and cut excess. **3.** Work Row 2 on back of piece. Begin by joining center of 200cm fishing line to end of Row 1, as shown in drawing. Pass fishing line through seed beads in Row 1 where indicated. Close circle. End in the same way as Row 1. **4.** Insert headpin into beads and bend. **5.** Attach clasp and headpin to ends of bracelet with jump rings.
Dimensions: 18cm long (end to end)

4
Headpin
Pearl bead (beige)
6-mm round glass bead

5
Clasp
Jump ring
Jump ring
Jump ring
Jump ring
Headpin

2

1.4-mm seed beads
2.7-mm seed beads
Jump ring
4-mm faceted glass bead (orange)
Bicone bead (brown)
4-mm faceted glass bead (purple)
6-mm faceted glass bead (green)
6-mm round glass bead
Bicone bead (orange)
6-mm faceted glass bead (orange)
4-mm faceted glass bead (purple)
Bicone bead (brown)

Tie ends together, hide in beads, and cut excess.

Center
1.5m fishing line
6-mm faceted glass bead (brown)
4-mm faceted glass bead (green)
Bicone bead (orange)
Bicone bead (brown)
Center
6-mm faceted glass bead (purple)
4-mm faceted glass bead (green)
4-mm faceted glass bead (orange)
Jump ring

3

200cm fishing line
★= 2.7-mm seed beads in Row 1
Pearl bead (purple)
Center
5 beads
7 beads
Pearl bead (beige)
☆= End here in same way as Row 1.
1.4-mm seed beads not shown.
Center

65

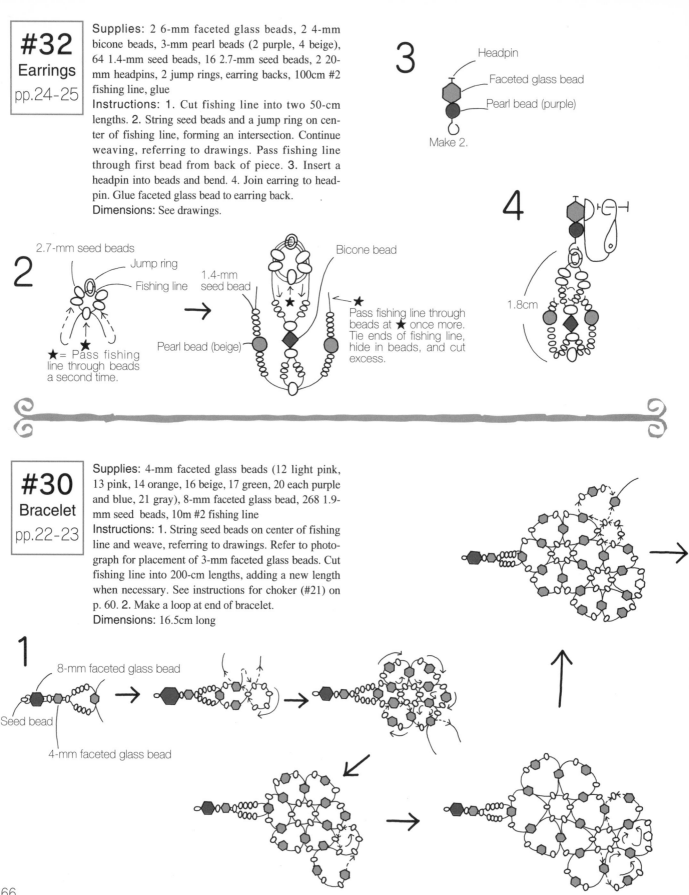

#32
Earrings
pp.24-25

Supplies: 2 6-mm faceted glass beads, 2 4-mm bicone beads, 3-mm pearl beads (2 purple, 4 beige), 64 1.4-mm seed beads, 16 2.7-mm seed beads, 2 20-mm headpins, 2 jump rings, earring backs, 100cm #2 fishing line, glue

Instructions: 1. Cut fishing line into two 50-cm lengths. 2. String seed beads and a jump ring on center of fishing line, forming an intersection. Continue weaving, referring to drawings. Pass fishing line through first bead from back of piece. 3. Insert a headpin into beads and bend. 4. Join earring to headpin. Glue faceted glass bead to earring back.

Dimensions: See drawings.

3

Headpin

Faceted glass bead

Pearl bead (purple)

Make 2.

2

2.7-mm seed beads

Jump ring

Fishing line

★ = Pass fishing line through beads a second time.

1.4-mm seed bead

Bicone bead

Pearl bead (beige)

★ Pass fishing line through beads at ★ once more. Tie ends of fishing line, hide in beads, and cut excess.

4

1.8cm

#30
Bracelet
pp.22-23

Supplies: 4-mm faceted glass beads (12 light pink, 13 pink, 14 orange, 16 beige, 17 green, 20 each purple and blue, 21 gray), 8-mm faceted glass bead, 268 1.9-mm seed beads, 10m #2 fishing line

Instructions: 1. String seed beads on center of fishing line and weave, referring to drawings. Refer to photograph for placement of 3-mm faceted glass beads. Cut fishing line into 200-cm lengths, adding a new length when necessary. See instructions for choker (#21) on p. 60. 2. Make a loop at end of bracelet.

Dimensions: 16.5cm long

1

8-mm faceted glass bead

Seed bead

4-mm faceted glass bead

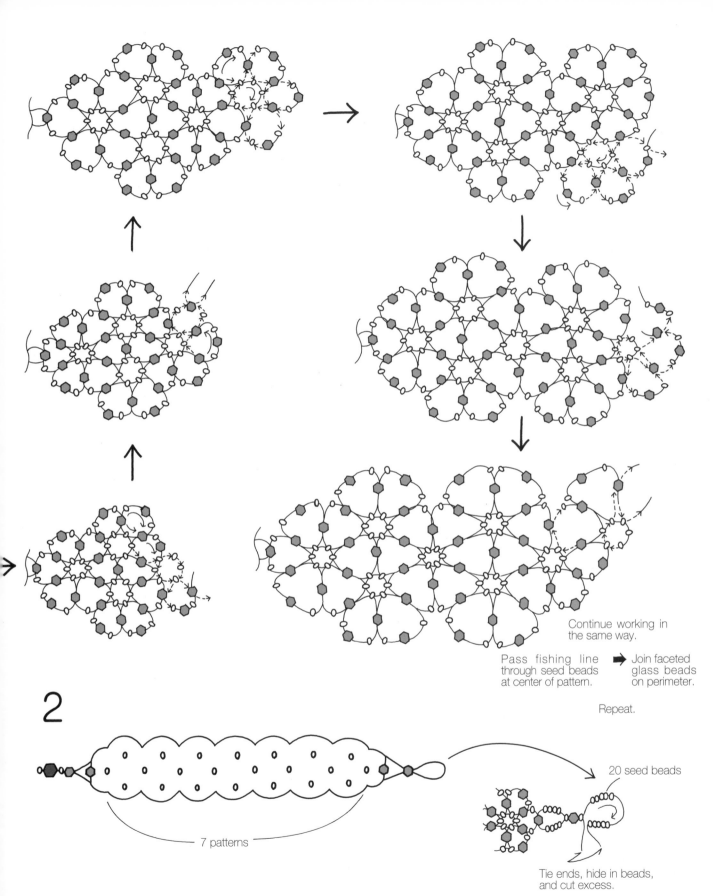

Continue working in
the same way.

Pass fishing line ➡ Join faceted
through seed beads   glass beads
at center of pattern.   on perimeter.

Repeat.

2

7 patterns

20 seed beads

Tie ends, hide in beads,
and cut excess.

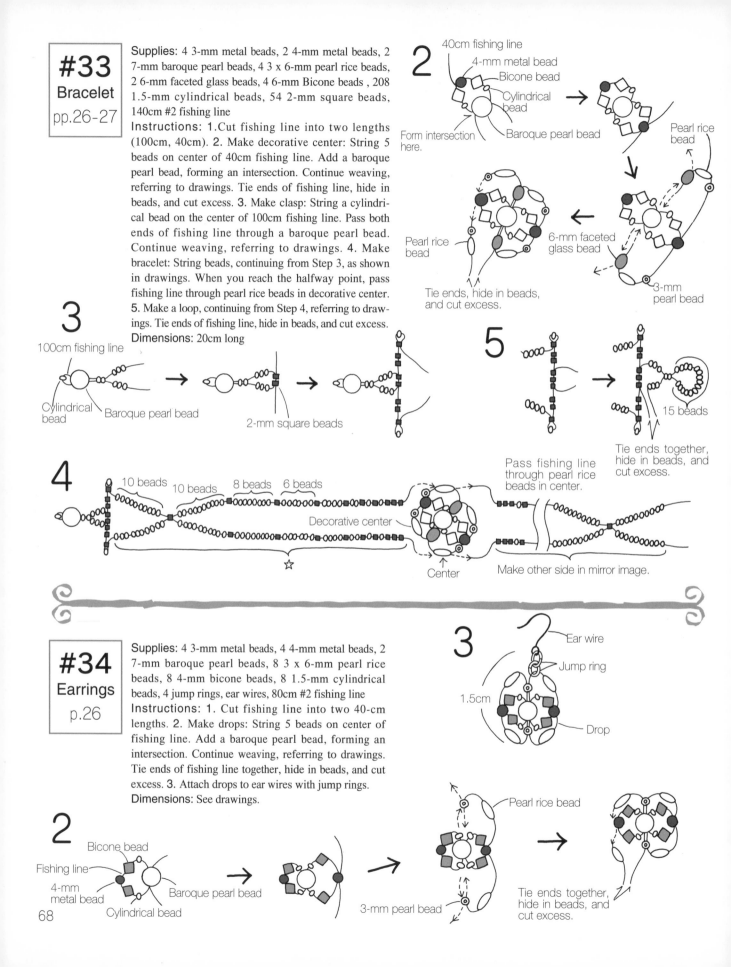

#33 Bracelet pp.26-27

Supplies: 4 3-mm metal beads, 2 4-mm metal beads, 2 7-mm baroque pearl beads, 4 3 x 6-mm pearl rice beads, 2 6-mm faceted glass beads, 4 6-mm Bicone beads , 208 1.5-mm cylindrical beads, 54 2-mm square beads, 140cm #2 fishing line

Instructions: 1.Cut fishing line into two lengths (100cm, 40cm). 2. Make decorative center: String 5 beads on center of 40cm fishing line. Add a baroque pearl bead, forming an intersection. Continue weaving, referring to drawings. Tie ends of fishing line, hide in beads, and cut excess. 3. Make clasp: String a cylindrical bead on the center of 100cm fishing line. Pass both ends of fishing line through a baroque pearl bead. Continue weaving, referring to drawings. 4. Make bracelet: String beads, continuing from Step 3, as shown in drawings. When you reach the halfway point, pass fishing line through pearl rice beads in decorative center. 5. Make a loop, continuing from Step 4, referring to drawings. Tie ends of fishing line, hide in beads, and cut excess.
Dimensions: 20cm long

2

40cm fishing line
4-mm metal bead
Bicone bead
Cylindrical bead
Form intersection here.
Baroque pearl bead
Pearl rice bead
6-mm faceted glass bead
3-mm pearl bead
Pearl rice bead
Tie ends, hide in beads, and cut excess.

3

100cm fishing line
Cylindrical bead
Baroque pearl bead
2-mm square beads

5

15 beads
Tie ends together, hide in beads, and cut excess.

4

10 beads   10 beads   8 beads   6 beads
Decorative center
☆
Center
Pass fishing line through pearl rice beads in center.
Make other side in mirror image.

#34 Earrings p.26

Supplies: 4 3-mm metal beads, 4 4-mm metal beads, 2 7-mm baroque pearl beads, 8 3 x 6-mm pearl rice beads, 8 4-mm bicone beads, 8 1.5-mm cylindrical beads, 4 jump rings, ear wires, 80cm #2 fishing line
Instructions: 1. Cut fishing line into two 40-cm lengths. 2. Make drops: String 5 beads on center of fishing line. Add a baroque pearl bead, forming an intersection. Continue weaving, referring to drawings. Tie ends of fishing line together, hide in beads, and cut excess. 3. Attach drops to ear wires with jump rings.
Dimensions: See drawings.

3

Ear wire
Jump ring
1.5cm
Drop

2

Bicone bead
Fishing line
4-mm metal bead
Cylindrical bead
Baroque pearl bead
3-mm pearl bead
Pearl rice bead
Tie ends together, hide in beads, and cut excess.

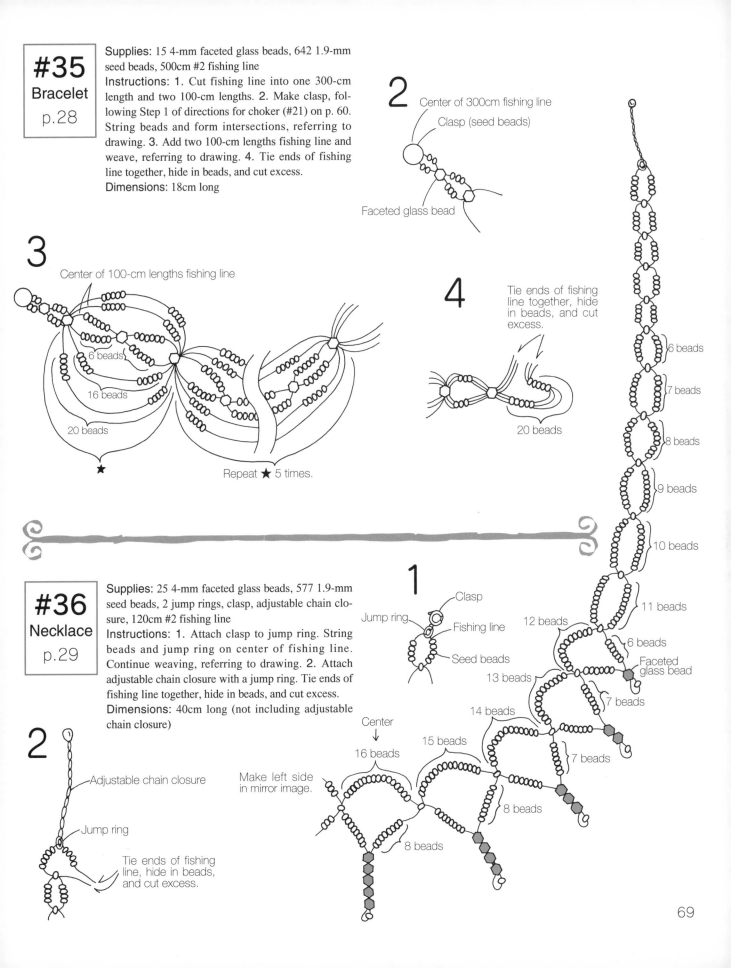

#35
Bracelet
p.28

Supplies: 15 4-mm faceted glass beads, 642 1.9-mm seed beads, 500cm #2 fishing line

Instructions: 1. Cut fishing line into one 300-cm length and two 100-cm lengths. 2. Make clasp, following Step 1 of directions for choker (#21) on p. 60. String beads and form intersections, referring to drawing. 3. Add two 100-cm lengths fishing line and weave, referring to drawing. 4. Tie ends of fishing line together, hide in beads, and cut excess.

Dimensions: 18cm long

2
Center of 300cm fishing line
Clasp (seed beads)
Faceted glass bead

3
Center of 100-cm lengths fishing line
6 beads
16 beads
20 beads
★
Repeat ★ 5 times.

4
Tie ends of fishing line together, hide in beads, and cut excess.
20 beads

#36
Necklace
p.29

Supplies: 25 4-mm faceted glass beads, 577 1.9-mm seed beads, 2 jump rings, clasp, adjustable chain closure, 120cm #2 fishing line

Instructions: 1. Attach clasp to jump ring. String beads and jump ring on center of fishing line. Continue weaving, referring to drawing. 2. Attach adjustable chain closure with a jump ring. Tie ends of fishing line together, hide in beads, and cut excess.

Dimensions: 40cm long (not including adjustable chain closure)

2
Adjustable chain closure
Jump ring
Tie ends of fishing line, hide in beads, and cut excess.

1
Clasp
Jump ring
Fishing line
Seed beads

6 beads
7 beads
8 beads
9 beads
10 beads
11 beads
6 beads
Faceted glass bead
12 beads
13 beads
7 beads
14 beads
7 beads
15 beads
8 beads
Center
16 beads
Make left side in mirror image.
8 beads

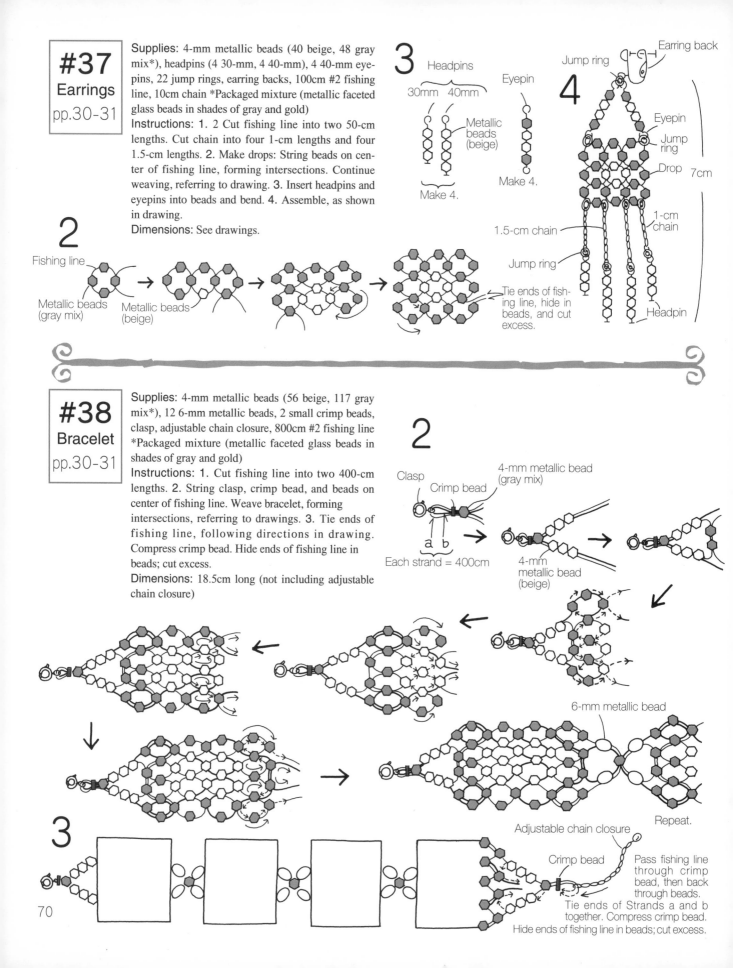

#37 Earrings
pp.30-31

Supplies: 4-mm metallic beads (40 beige, 48 gray mix*), headpins (4 30-mm, 4 40-mm), 4 40-mm eyepins, 22 jump rings, earring backs, 100cm #2 fishing line, 10cm chain *Packaged mixture (metallic faceted glass beads in shades of gray and gold)

Instructions: 1. 2 Cut fishing line into two 50-cm lengths. Cut chain into four 1-cm lengths and four 1.5-cm lengths. 2. Make drops: String beads on center of fishing line, forming intersections. Continue weaving, referring to drawing. 3. Insert headpins and eyepins into beads and bend. 4. Assemble, as shown in drawing.

Dimensions: See drawings.

3 Headpins
30mm 40mm
Metallic beads (beige)
Make 4.
Eyepin
Metallic beads (beige)
Make 4.

4
Jump ring
Earring back
Eyepin
Jump ring
Drop 7cm
1-cm chain
1.5-cm chain
Jump ring
Headpin

2
Fishing line
Metallic beads (gray mix)
Metallic beads (beige)
Tie ends of fishing line, hide in beads, and cut excess.

#38 Bracelet
pp.30-31

Supplies: 4-mm metallic beads (56 beige, 117 gray mix*), 12 6-mm metallic beads, 2 small crimp beads, clasp, adjustable chain closure, 800cm #2 fishing line *Packaged mixture (metallic faceted glass beads in shades of gray and gold)

Instructions: 1. Cut fishing line into two 400-cm lengths. 2. String clasp, crimp bead, and beads on center of fishing line. Weave bracelet, forming intersections, referring to drawings. 3. Tie ends of fishing line, following directions in drawing. Compress crimp bead. Hide ends of fishing line in beads; cut excess.

Dimensions: 18.5cm long (not including adjustable chain closure)

2
Clasp
Crimp bead
4-mm metallic bead (gray mix)
a b
Each strand = 400cm
4-mm metallic bead (beige)
6-mm metallic bead
Repeat.

3
Adjustable chain closure
Crimp bead
Pass fishing line through crimp bead, then back through beads. Tie ends of Strands a and b together. Compress crimp bead. Hide ends of fishing line in beads; cut excess.

70

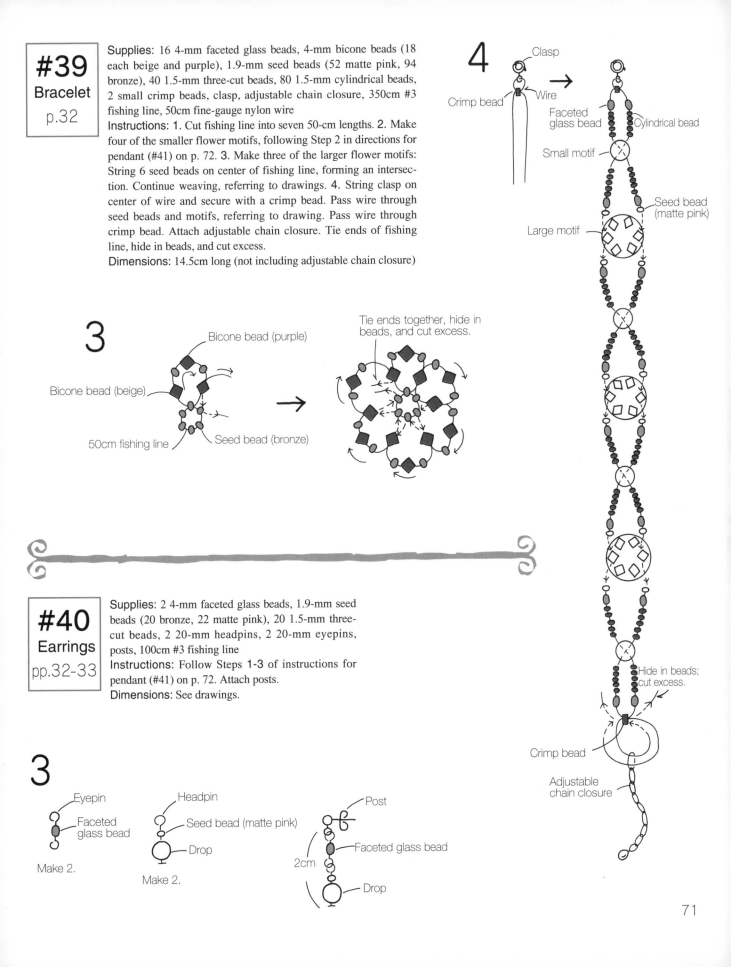

#39 Bracelet
p.32

Supplies: 16 4-mm faceted glass beads, 4-mm bicone beads (18 each beige and purple), 1.9-mm seed beads (52 matte pink, 94 bronze), 40 1.5-mm three-cut beads, 80 1.5-mm cylindrical beads, 2 small crimp beads, clasp, adjustable chain closure, 350cm #3 fishing line, 50cm fine-gauge nylon wire

Instructions: 1. Cut fishing line into seven 50-cm lengths. **2.** Make four of the smaller flower motifs, following Step 2 in directions for pendant (#41) on p. 72. **3.** Make three of the larger flower motifs: String 6 seed beads on center of fishing line, forming an intersection. Continue weaving, referring to drawings. **4.** String clasp on center of wire and secure with a crimp bead. Pass wire through seed beads and motifs, referring to drawing. Pass wire through crimp bead. Attach adjustable chain closure. Tie ends of fishing line, hide in beads, and cut excess.

Dimensions: 14.5cm long (not including adjustable chain closure)

3

Bicone bead (purple)

Bicone bead (beige)

50cm fishing line

Seed bead (bronze)

Tie ends together, hide in beads, and cut excess.

4

Clasp

Crimp bead

Wire

Faceted glass bead

Cylindrical bead

Small motif

Seed bead (matte pink)

Large motif

Hide in beads; cut excess.

Crimp bead

Adjustable chain closure

#40 Earrings
pp.32-33

Supplies: 2 4-mm faceted glass beads, 1.9-mm seed beads (20 bronze, 22 matte pink), 20 1.5-mm three-cut beads, 2 20-mm headpins, 2 20-mm eyepins, posts, 100cm #3 fishing line

Instructions: Follow Steps 1-3 of instructions for pendant (#41) on p. 72. Attach posts.

Dimensions: See drawings.

3

Eyepin

Faceted glass bead

Make 2.

Headpin

Seed bead (matte pink)

Drop

Make 2.

Post

Faceted glass bead

2cm

Drop

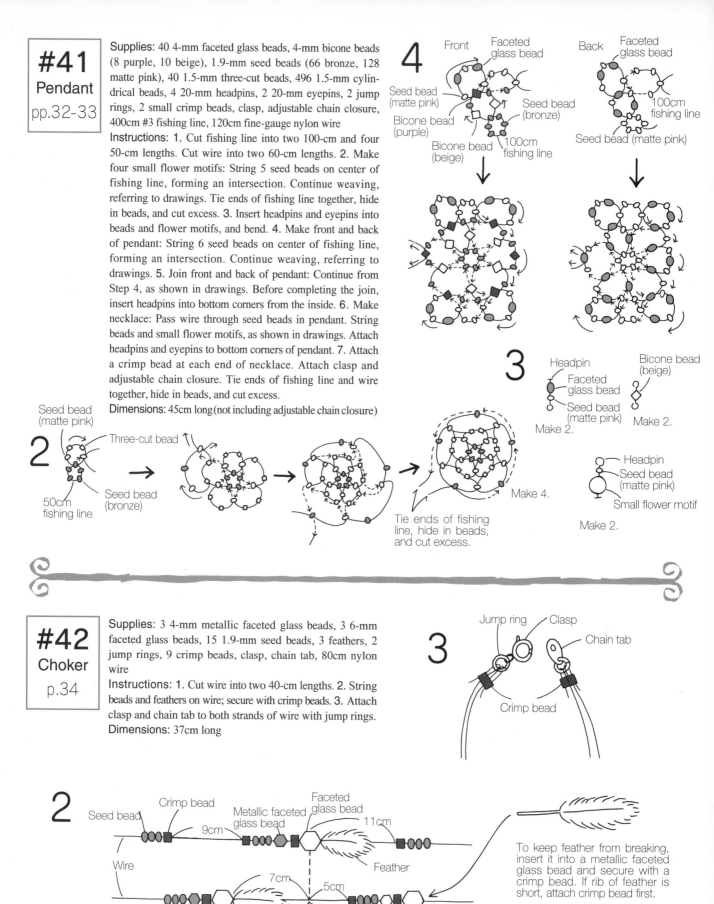

#41 Pendant
pp.32-33

Supplies: 40 4-mm faceted glass beads, 4-mm bicone beads (8 purple, 10 beige), 1.9-mm seed beads (66 bronze, 128 matte pink), 40 1.5-mm three-cut beads, 496 1.5-mm cylindrical beads, 4 20-mm headpins, 2 20-mm eyepins, 2 jump rings, 2 small crimp beads, clasp, adjustable chain closure, 400cm #3 fishing line, 120cm fine-gauge nylon wire

Instructions: 1. Cut fishing line into two 100-cm and four 50-cm lengths. Cut wire into two 60-cm lengths. 2. Make four small flower motifs: String 5 seed beads on center of fishing line, forming an intersection. Continue weaving, referring to drawings. Tie ends of fishing line together, hide in beads, and cut excess. 3. Insert headpins and eyepins into beads and flower motifs, and bend. 4. Make front and back of pendant: String 6 seed beads on center of fishing line, forming an intersection. Continue weaving, referring to drawings. 5. Join front and back of pendant: Continue from Step 4, as shown in drawings. Before completing the join, insert headpins into bottom corners from the inside. 6. Make necklace: Pass wire through seed beads in pendant. String beads and small flower motifs, as shown in drawings. Attach headpins and eyepins to bottom corners of pendant. 7. Attach a crimp bead at each end of necklace. Attach clasp and adjustable chain closure. Tie ends of fishing line and wire together, hide in beads, and cut excess.

Dimensions: 45cm long (not including adjustable chain closure)

4 Front — Faceted glass bead / Back — Faceted glass bead

Seed bead (matte pink) / Seed bead (bronze) / Bicone bead (purple) / Bicone bead (beige) / 100cm fishing line / Seed bead (matte pink) / 100cm fishing line

3 Headpin / Faceted glass bead / Seed bead (matte pink) / Make 2. / Bicone bead (beige) / Make 2.

Headpin / Seed bead (matte pink) / Small flower motif / Make 2.

2 Seed bead (matte pink) / Three-cut bead / 50cm fishing line / Seed bead (bronze) / Tie ends of fishing line, hide in beads, and cut excess. / Make 4.

#42 Choker
p.34

Supplies: 3 4-mm metallic faceted glass beads, 3 6-mm faceted glass beads, 15 1.9-mm seed beads, 3 feathers, 2 jump rings, 9 crimp beads, clasp, chain tab, 80cm nylon wire

Instructions: 1. Cut wire into two 40-cm lengths. 2. String beads and feathers on wire; secure with crimp beads. 3. Attach clasp and chain tab to both strands of wire with jump rings.

Dimensions: 37cm long

3 Jump ring / Clasp / Chain tab / Crimp bead

2 Seed bead / Crimp bead / Metallic faceted glass bead / Faceted glass bead / 11cm / 9cm / Feather / Wire / 7cm / 5cm / Center

To keep feather from breaking, insert it into a metallic faceted glass bead and secure with a crimp bead. If rib of feather is short, attach crimp bead first.

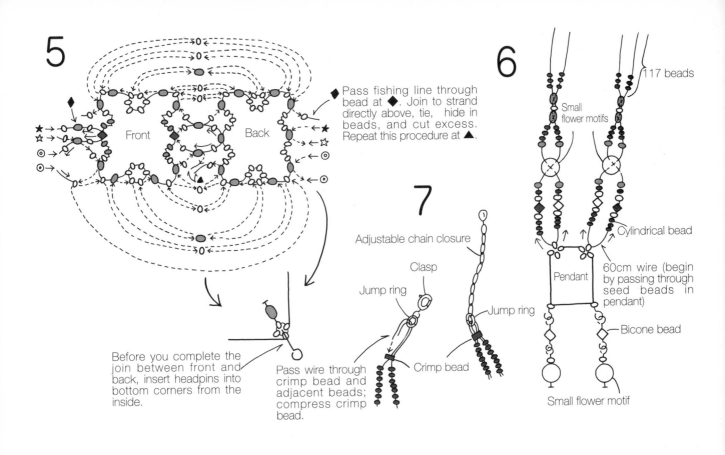

5

Front   Back

♦ Pass fishing line through bead at ♦. Join to strand directly above, tie, hide in beads, and cut excess. Repeat this procedure at ▲.

Before you complete the join between front and back, insert headpins into bottom corners from the inside.

Pass wire through crimp bead and adjacent beads; compress crimp bead.

7

Adjustable chain closure

Clasp

Jump ring

Jump ring

Crimp bead

6

117 beads

Small flower motifs

Cylindrical bead

60cm wire (begin by passing through seed beads in pendant)

Pendant

Bicone bead

Small flower motif

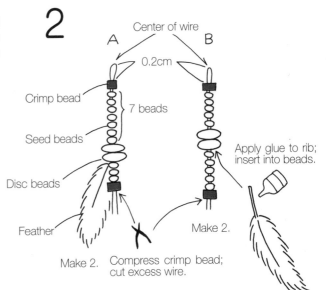

#44
Earrings
p.35

Supplies: 8 6-mm disc beads, 40 1.9-mm seed beads, 4 feathers, 2 jump rings, 8 small crimp beads, ear wires, 40cm fine-gauge nylon wire, glue

Instructions: 1. Cut wire into four 10-cm lengths. 2. Bend wire in half and string beads. Attach feathers and secure with glue and crimp beads. 3. Attach ear wires with jump rings.

Dimensions: See drawings.

2

Center of wire

A   B

0.2cm

Crimp bead

7 beads

Seed beads

Disc beads

Apply glue to rib; insert into beads.

Feather

Make 2.

Make 2.   Compress crimp bead; cut excess wire.

3

Ear wire

Jump ring

4.5cm

A

B

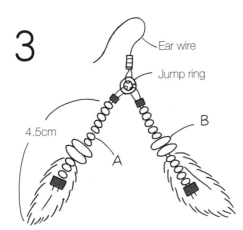

#43 Bracelet
p.35

Supplies: 16 6-mm disc beads, 266 1.9-mm seed beads, 8 feathers, 14 20-mm eyepins, 2 jump rings, 6 small crimp beads, clasp, chain tab, 65cm nylon wire, glue

Instructions: 1. Cut wire into one 25-cm length and two 20-cm lengths. 2. Insert eyepin into seed beads and bend. 3. String beads on wire. Attach feathers with glue and crimp beads. 4. Join sections shown in Figs. 2 and 3 with eyepins. 5. Attach clasp and chain tab with jump rings.

Dimensions: 16.5cm long

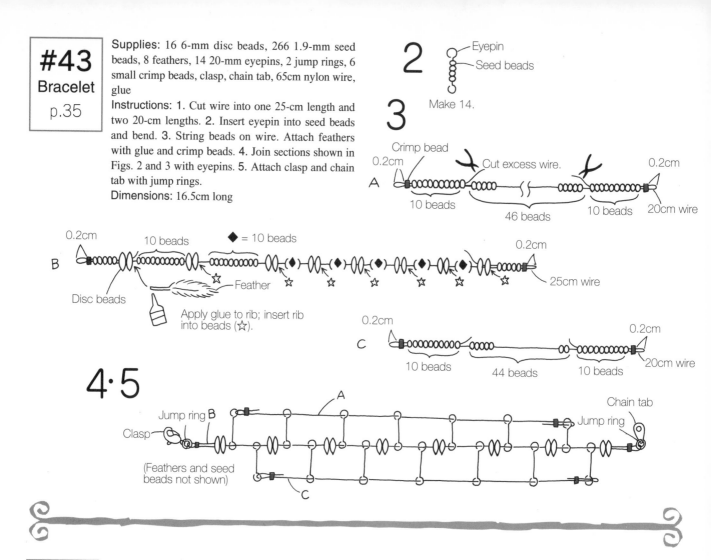

2 Eyepin / Seed beads
Make 14.

3
Crimp bead
0.2cm   Cut excess wire.   0.2cm
A   10 beads   46 beads   10 beads   20cm wire

B   0.2cm   10 beads   ◆ = 10 beads   0.2cm
Disc beads   ☆   Feather   ☆ ☆ ☆ ☆ ☆ ☆   25cm wire
Apply glue to rib; insert rib into beads (☆).

C   0.2cm   0.2cm
10 beads   44 beads   10 beads   20cm wire

4·5
Jump ring B   A   Chain tab
Clasp   Jump ring
(Feathers and seed beads not shown)   C

#45 Necklace
pp.36–37

Supplies: 12 4-mm glass beads, 583 1.5-mm three-cut beads, 496 1.5-mm cylindrical beads, seed beads (527 1.4-mm, 70 1.9-mm, 36 2.7-mm beads), 12 15-mm headpins, 35 35-mm eyepins, 41 jump rings, 6 small crimp beads, clasp, adjustable chain closure, 10.2m fine-gauge nylon wire

Instructions: 1. Cut wire into two 25-cm lengths, 29 30-cm lengths, and two 50-cm lengths. 2. Make 29 of the 20 types of leaves: String beads on center of wire, forming intersections. Finish each leaf as shown in drawing, cut excess wire, and attach a jump ring. 3. Make pieces that extend from bottom to top of necklace by inserting eyepins into beads and bending the ends. 4. Attach 25cm wire to two eyepins. String cylindrical beads on wire. 5. Insert two 50-cm strands wire and one strand wire from Step 4 into clasmp. Secure with a crimp bead. String beads on 50cm wire. 6. Pass wire through leaves, headpins, and beads, referring to drawing. Pass three strands wire from Step 4 through opening in adjustable chain closure. Secure with crimp bead.

Dimensions: 32cm long (not including adjustable chain closure)

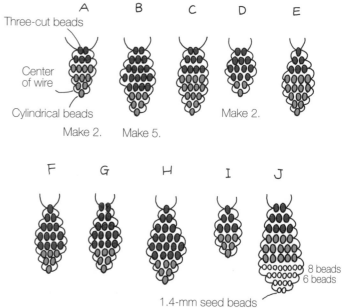

2   A   B   C   D   E
Three-cut beads
Center of wire
Cylindrical beads   Make 2.
Make 2.   Make 5.

F   G   H   I   J
8 beads
6 beads
1.4-mm seed beads

74

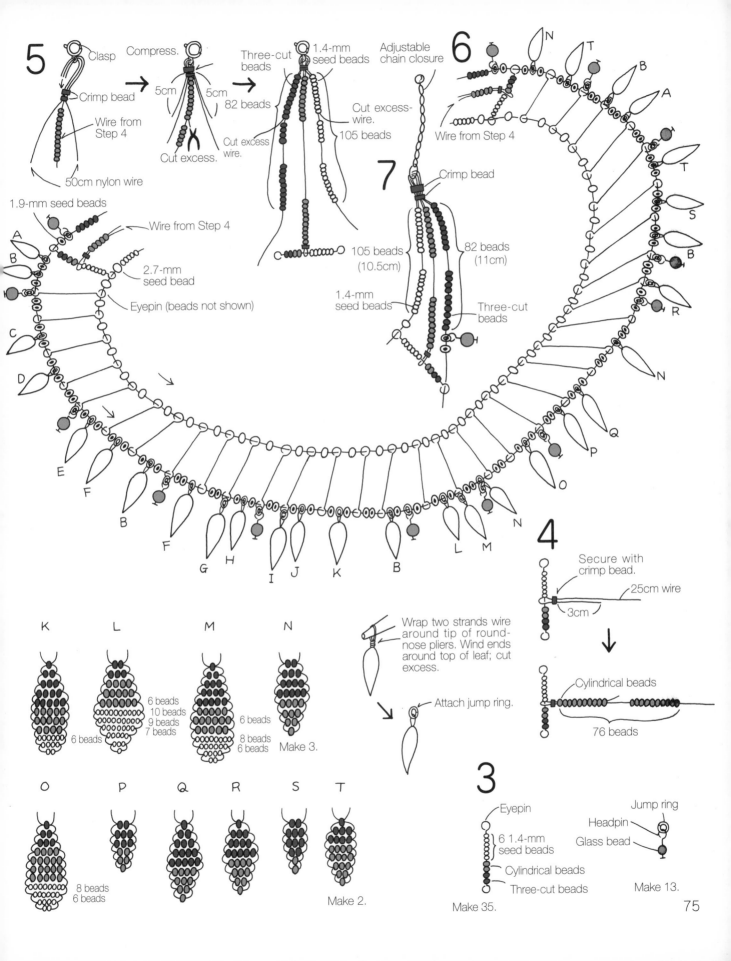

5
Clasp
Compress.
Three-cut beads
1.4-mm seed beads
Adjustable chain closure
Crimp bead
Wire from Step 4
5cm   5cm
82 beads
Cut excess wire.
105 beads
Wire from Step 4
Wire from Step 4
Cut excess.
Cut excess wire.
50cm nylon wire

6

1.9-mm seed beads
Wire from Step 4
2.7-mm seed bead
Eyepin (beads not shown)

7
Crimp bead
105 beads (10.5cm)
82 beads (11cm)
1.4-mm seed beads
Three-cut beads

A B C D E F B F G H I J K B L M N O P Q R S T N

Wrap two strands wire around tip of round-nose pliers. Wind ends around top of leaf; cut excess.

Attach jump ring.

4
Secure with crimp bead.
25cm wire
3cm
Cylindrical beads
76 beads

K — 6 beads / 6 beads

L — 6 beads / 10 beads / 9 beads / 7 beads

M — 6 beads / 8 beads / 6 beads

N — Make 3.

O — 8 beads / 6 beads

P Q R S T — Make 2.

3
Eyepin
6 1.4-mm seed beads
Cylindrical beads
Three-cut beads
Make 35.

Jump ring
Headpin
Glass bead
Make 13.

75

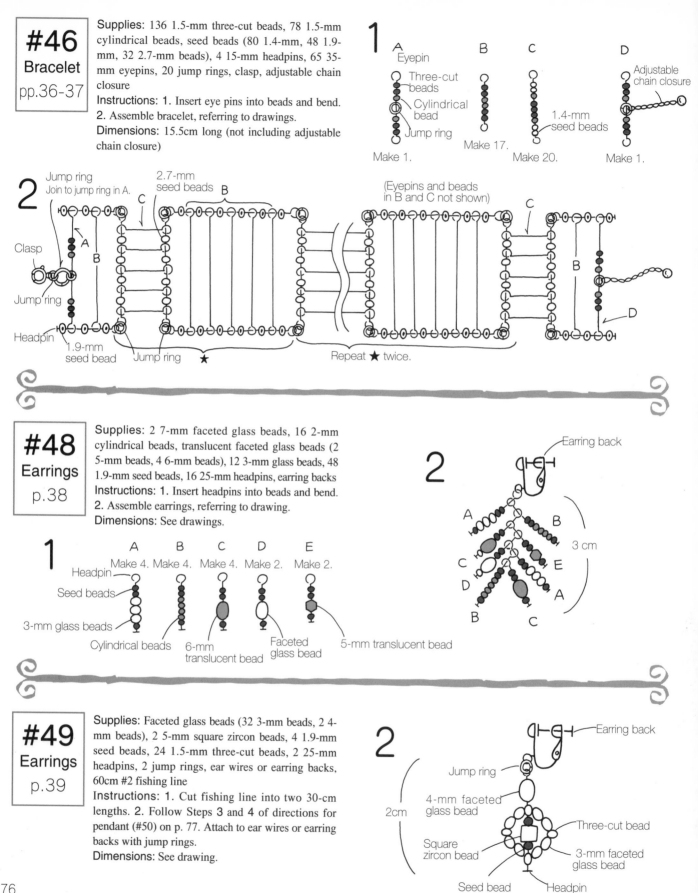

#46 Bracelet
pp.36-37

Supplies: 136 1.5-mm three-cut beads, 78 1.5-mm cylindrical beads, seed beads (80 1.4-mm, 48 1.9-mm, 32 2.7-mm beads), 4 15-mm headpins, 65 35-mm eyepins, 20 jump rings, clasp, adjustable chain closure

Instructions: 1. Insert eye pins into beads and bend. 2. Assemble bracelet, referring to drawings.

Dimensions: 15.5cm long (not including adjustable chain closure)

1

A Eyepin Three-cut beads Cylindrical bead Jump ring **Make 1.**

B **Make 17.**

C 1.4-mm seed beads **Make 20.**

D Adjustable chain closure **Make 1.**

2 Jump ring Join to jump ring in A. 2.7-mm seed beads C B A B (Eyepins and beads in B and C not shown) C B D

Clasp Jump ring Headpin 1.9-mm seed bead Jump ring ★ Repeat ★ twice.

#48 Earrings
p.38

Supplies: 2 7-mm faceted glass beads, 16 2-mm cylindrical beads, translucent faceted glass beads (2 5-mm beads, 4 6-mm beads), 12 3-mm glass beads, 48 1.9-mm seed beads, 16 25-mm headpins, earring backs

Instructions: 1. Insert headpins into beads and bend. 2. Assemble earrings, referring to drawing.

Dimensions: See drawings.

1 A **Make 4.** B **Make 4.** C **Make 4.** D **Make 2.** E **Make 2.**

Headpin Seed beads 3-mm glass beads Cylindrical beads 6-mm translucent bead Faceted glass bead 5-mm translucent bead

2 Earring back A B C E D A B C 3 cm

#49 Earrings
p.39

Supplies: Faceted glass beads (32 3-mm beads, 2 4-mm beads), 2 5-mm square zircon beads, 4 1.9-mm seed beads, 24 1.5-mm three-cut beads, 2 25-mm headpins, 2 jump rings, ear wires or earring backs, 60cm #2 fishing line

Instructions: 1. Cut fishing line into two 30-cm lengths. 2. Follow Steps 3 and 4 of directions for pendant (#50) on p. 77. Attach to ear wires or earring backs with jump rings.

Dimensions: See drawing.

2 Earring back Jump ring 4-mm faceted glass bead 2cm Square zircon bead Three-cut bead 3-mm faceted glass bead Seed bead Headpin

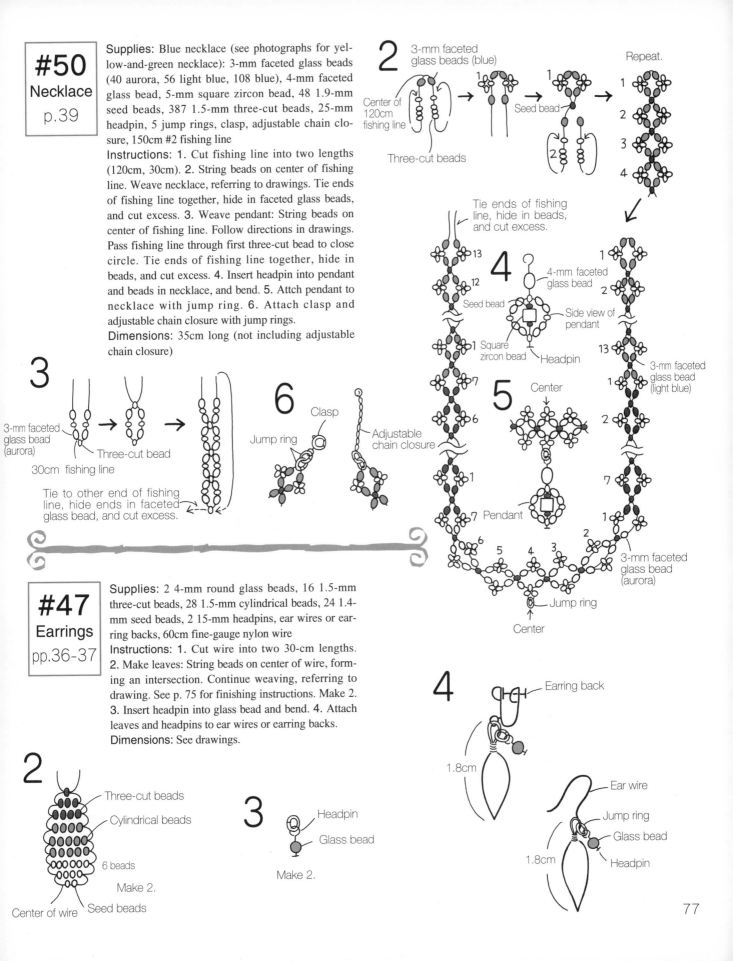

#50 Necklace p.39

Supplies: Blue necklace (see photographs for yellow-and-green necklace): 3-mm faceted glass beads (40 aurora, 56 light blue, 108 blue), 4-mm faceted glass bead, 5-mm square zircon bead, 48 1.9-mm seed beads, 387 1.5-mm three-cut beads, 25-mm headpin, 5 jump rings, clasp, adjustable chain closure, 150cm #2 fishing line

Instructions: 1. Cut fishing line into two lengths (120cm, 30cm). 2. String beads on center of fishing line. Weave necklace, referring to drawings. Tie ends of fishing line together, hide in faceted glass beads, and cut excess. 3. Weave pendant: String beads on center of fishing line. Follow directions in drawings. Pass fishing line through first three-cut bead to close circle. Tie ends of fishing line together, hide in beads, and cut excess. 4. Insert headpin into pendant and beads in necklace, and bend. 5. Attch pendant to necklace with jump ring. 6. Attach clasp and adjustable chain closure with jump rings.

Dimensions: 35cm long (not including adjustable chain closure)

2 3-mm faceted glass beads (blue)

Center of 120cm fishing line

Three-cut beads

Seed bead

Repeat.

Tie ends of fishing line, hide in beads, and cut excess.

4 4-mm faceted glass bead

Seed bead

Square zircon bead

Side view of pendant

Headpin

3 3-mm faceted glass bead (aurora)

Three-cut bead

30cm fishing line

Tie to other end of fishing line, hide ends in faceted glass bead, and cut excess.

6 Clasp

Jump ring

Adjustable chain closure

5 Center

Pendant

Jump ring

Center

3-mm faceted glass bead (light blue)

3-mm faceted glass bead (aurora)

#47 Earrings pp.36-37

Supplies: 2 4-mm round glass beads, 16 1.5-mm three-cut beads, 28 1.5-mm cylindrical beads, 24 1.4-mm seed beads, 2 15-mm headpins, ear wires or earring backs, 60cm fine-gauge nylon wire

Instructions: 1. Cut wire into two 30-cm lengths. 2. Make leaves: String beads on center of wire, forming an intersection. Continue weaving, referring to drawing. See p. 75 for finishing instructions. Make 2. 3. Insert headpin into glass bead and bend. 4. Attach leaves and headpins to ear wires or earring backs.

Dimensions: See drawings.

2 Three-cut beads

Cylindrical beads

6 beads

Make 2.

Center of wire   Seed beads

3 Headpin

Glass bead

Make 2.

4 Earring back

1.8cm

Ear wire

Jump ring

Glass bead

Headpin

1.8cm

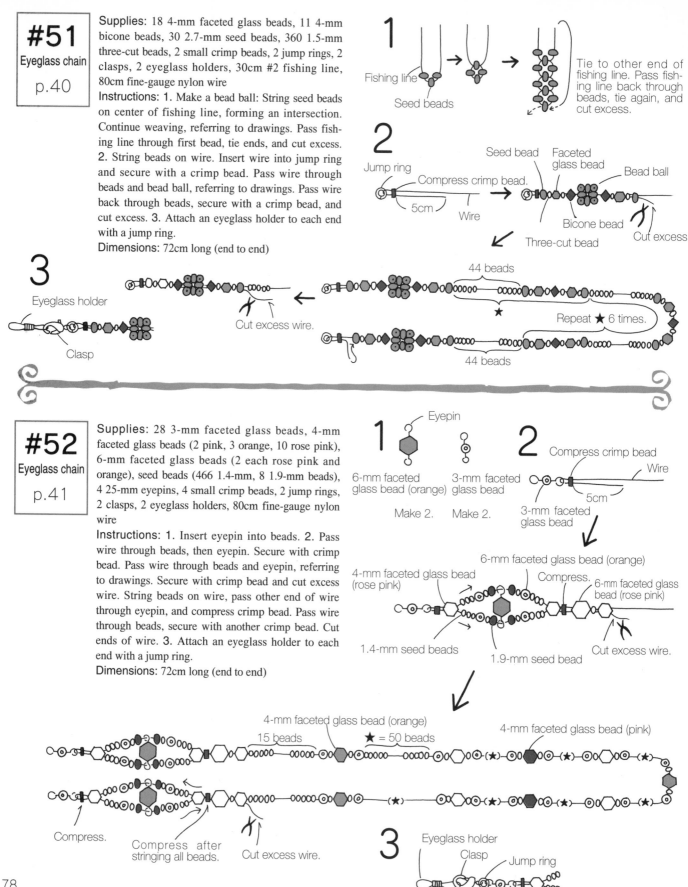

#51 Eyeglass chain p.40

Supplies: 18 4-mm faceted glass beads, 11 4-mm bicone beads, 30 2.7-mm seed beads, 360 1.5-mm three-cut beads, 2 small crimp beads, 2 jump rings, 2 clasps, 2 eyeglass holders, 30cm #2 fishing line, 80cm fine-gauge nylon wire

Instructions: 1. Make a bead ball: String seed beads on center of fishing line, forming an intersection. Continue weaving, referring to drawings. Pass fishing line through first bead, tie ends, and cut excess. 2. String beads on wire. Insert wire into jump ring and secure with a crimp bead. Pass wire through beads and bead ball, referring to drawings. Pass wire back through beads, secure with a crimp bead, and cut excess. 3. Attach an eyeglass holder to each end with a jump ring.

Dimensions: 72cm long (end to end)

1
Fishing line
Seed beads
Tie to other end of fishing line. Pass fishing line back through beads, tie again, and cut excess.

2
Jump ring
Compress crimp bead.
5cm
Wire
Seed bead
Faceted glass bead
Bead ball
Bicone bead
Three-cut bead
Cut excess.

3
Eyeglass holder
Clasp
Cut excess wire.
44 beads
★
Repeat ★ 6 times.
44 beads

#52 Eyeglass chain p.41

Supplies: 28 3-mm faceted glass beads, 4-mm faceted glass beads (2 pink, 3 orange, 10 rose pink), 6-mm faceted glass beads (2 each rose pink and orange), seed beads (466 1.4-mm, 8 1.9-mm beads), 4 25-mm eyepins, 4 small crimp beads, 2 jump rings, 2 clasps, 2 eyeglass holders, 80cm fine-gauge nylon wire

Instructions: 1. Insert eyepin into beads. 2. Pass wire through beads, then eyepin. Secure with crimp bead. Pass wire through beads and eyepin, referring to drawings. Secure with crimp bead and cut excess wire. String beads on wire, pass other end of wire through eyepin, and compress crimp bead. Pass wire through beads, secure with another crimp bead. Cut ends of wire. 3. Attach an eyeglass holder to each end with a jump ring.

Dimensions: 72cm long (end to end)

1
Eyepin
6-mm faceted glass bead (orange)
Make 2.
3-mm faceted glass bead
Make 2.

2
Compress crimp bead.
Wire
5cm
3-mm faceted glass bead
4-mm faceted glass bead (rose pink)
6-mm faceted glass bead (orange)
Compress.
6-mm faceted glass bead (rose pink)
1.4-mm seed beads
1.9-mm seed bead
Cut excess wire.

4-mm faceted glass bead (orange)
15 beads
★ = 50 beads
4-mm faceted glass bead (pink)
Compress.
Compress after stringing all beads.
Cut excess wire.

3
Eyeglass holder
Clasp
Jump ring

#53 Cell phone strap
p.41

Supplies: Faceted glass beads (9 3-mm beads, 1 5-mm bead), 8-mm disc bead, 43 1.9-mm seed beads, strap, 3 crimp beads, 30cm #2 fishing line, 30cm nylon wire

Instructions: 1. String a bead and a crimp bead 8cm from one end of wire. Pass end of wire back through crimp bead and compress (see drawing). 2. String beads on fishing line and wire. Finish as directed in Step 1. 3. Pass wire through faceted glass beads. Gather two strands of wire and insert into a crimp bead, faceted glass bead, and strap. Compress crimp bead; cut excess wire.

Dimensions: 16.5cm long

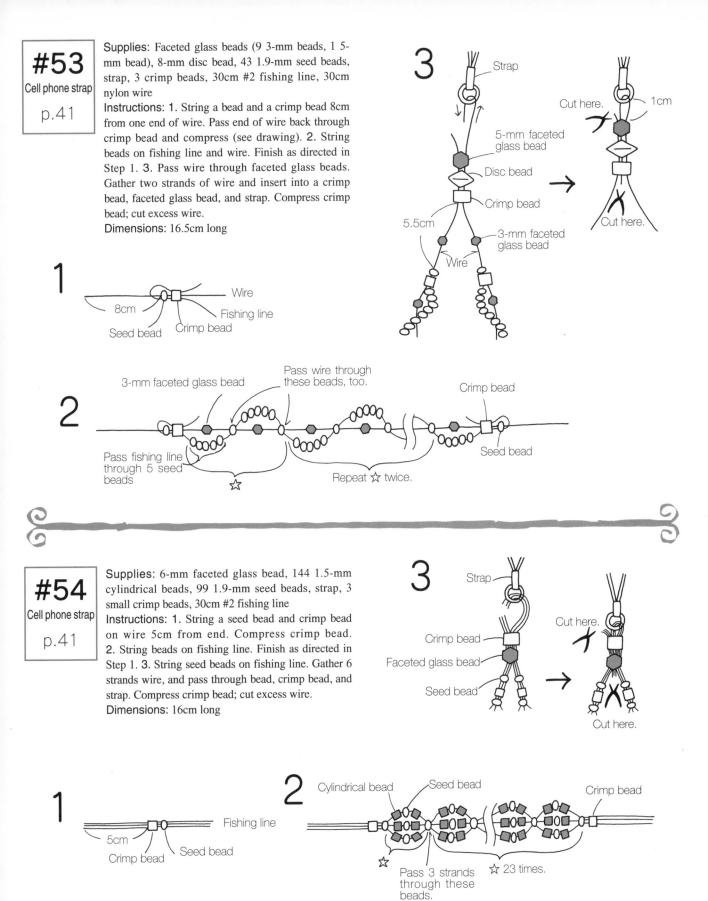

3
Strap
5-mm faceted glass bead
Disc bead
Crimp bead
5.5cm
3-mm faceted glass bead
Wire
Cut here.
1cm
Cut here.

1
Wire
8cm
Fishing line
Seed bead
Crimp bead

2
3-mm faceted glass bead
Pass wire through these beads, too.
Crimp bead
Pass fishing line through 5 seed beads
Seed bead
Repeat ☆ twice.
☆

#54 Cell phone strap
p.41

Supplies: 6-mm faceted glass bead, 144 1.5-mm cylindrical beads, 99 1.9-mm seed beads, strap, 3 small crimp beads, 30cm #2 fishing line

Instructions: 1. String a seed bead and crimp bead on wire 5cm from end. Compress crimp bead. 2. String beads on fishing line. Finish as directed in Step 1. 3. String seed beads on fishing line. Gather 6 strands wire, and pass through bead, crimp bead, and strap. Compress crimp bead; cut excess wire.

Dimensions: 16cm long

3
Strap
Crimp bead
Faceted glass bead
Seed bead
Cut here.
Cut here.

1
Fishing line
5cm
Crimp bead
Seed bead

2
Cylindrical bead
Seed bead
Crimp bead
☆
Pass 3 strands through these beads.
☆ 23 times.

#8
Ring
p.9

Supplies: Brown ring (see photograph for red ring): 4-mm faceted glass beads (22 each brown and dark brown), 5 4-mm metallic beads, seed beads (32 1.4-mm, 50 1.9-mm beads), 150cm #3 fishing line

Instructions: String beads on center of fishing line, forming an intersection. Continue weaving, referring to drawings. Close circle after you have worked four patterns. Tie ends of fishing line together, hide in beads, and cut excess.

Dimensions: 5.5cm (inside diameter)

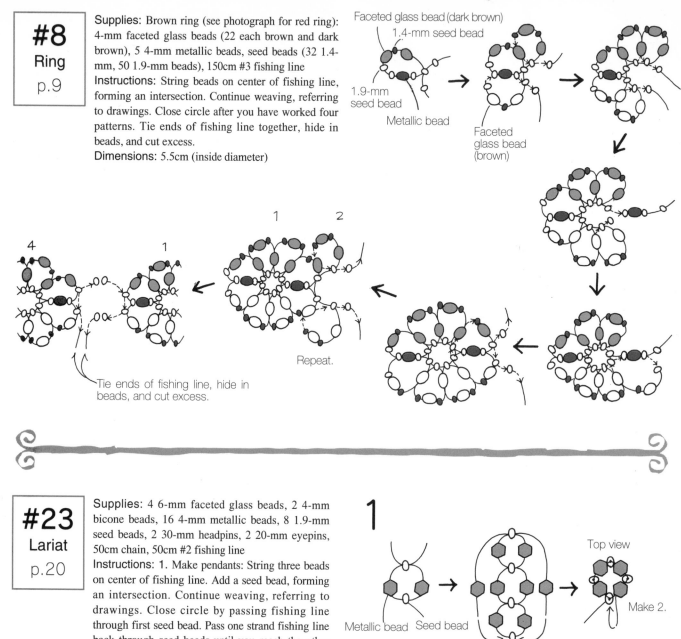

Faceted glass bead (dark brown)
1.4-mm seed bead
1.9-mm seed bead
Metallic bead
Faceted glass bead (brown)

Repeat.

Tie ends of fishing line, hide in beads, and cut excess.

#23
Lariat
p.20

Supplies: 4 6-mm faceted glass beads, 2 4-mm bicone beads, 16 4-mm metallic beads, 8 1.9-mm seed beads, 2 30-mm headpins, 2 20-mm eyepins, 50cm chain, 50cm #2 fishing line

Instructions: 1. Make pendants: String three beads on center of fishing line. Add a seed bead, forming an intersection. Continue weaving, referring to drawings. Close circle by passing fishing line through first seed bead. Pass one strand fishing line back through seed beads until you reach the other strand. Tie ends together, hide in beads, and cut excess. 2. Insert headpins and eyepins into pendants and bend. 3. Attach chain to pendants.

Dimensions: 58cm (end to end)

1

Metallic bead   Seed bead

Top view

Make 2.

2

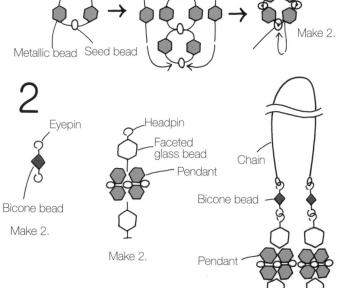

Eyepin

Bicone bead

Make 2.

Headpin
Faceted glass bead
Pendant

Make 2.

Chain

Bicone bead

Pendant